The Swedish Christmas Table

Made in
Sweden

Jens Linder and Johanna Westman

The Swedish Christmas Table

Traditional Holiday Meals, Side Dishes, Candies, and Drinks

Translated by River Khan

Photography by Ulrika Pousette Collages by Pia Koskela

Skyhorse Publishing

SATURNUS

Saturnus
CITRON
DROPPAR

HUSHÅLL
DROPPAR

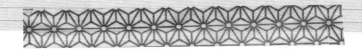

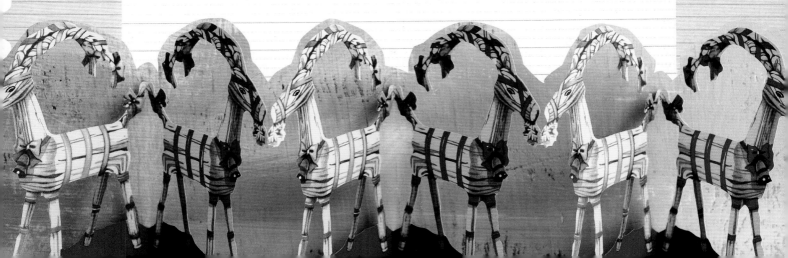

Foreword

Oh, beautiful Christmas!

We are two Christmas nerds who love great and sensational flavors, who thrive among ladles and casseroles, and who gladly throw the holiday parties. On the outside, we probably appear quite different from one another. Jens gladly digs deep into the lovely heritage of our Swedish food as well as into the kitchens of other cultures, and he doesn't balk at any part of the animal. Johanna is constantly looking for new flavors and dishes that are both childishly simple and inventive, but often ends up in the Italian saucepan—and is quite happy there.

The love for clean and lovingly cooked food unites us. We have both been writing about food for the past century and our passion for food reaches its devoted, joyful peak every month of December when gluttony and revelry are socially acceptable and the spirit of tradition is strong.

Our collaboration first began in 2010 when we were asked to do a food report together for a monthly magazine. We were told to write about Christmas, food, and crafts and preferably with some happy innovation. During our very first tentative meeting we hatched the idea to make a wreath out of a metal clothes hanger—and there have since been a number of very giggly meetings.

It wasn't long before we began to dream about doing a book together. A Christmas book where everything would find room: the traditional and the modern, classic parade dishes and new dishes where seasonal ingredients would be put to the best use—sweet, savory, strong, and fresh. A book in which all the highlights of the month of December would be included—everything from baked dishes to advent breakfast to something to munch on when you ring in the new year. We've had loads of fun along the way! And now you're holding our combined Christmas dream!

We wish you and yours
a merry Christmas, a happy
new year, and a lot of
tasty treats in between!

Jens and Johanna

WREATHS

Make a different kind of Christmas wreath in 10 minutes with the help of a metal clothes hanger.

You need: metal clothes hanger, saffron buns.

Bend the hanger into a circle. Use wire cutters to cut open the circle at one side of the hanger's hook. Thread the most Christmassy thing you can find at home on to it. Why not some saffron buns from the freezer? Leave a few inches of the metal wire free, so you can close up the circle and the wreath is ready to be hung up.

December

1
Make a thorough Christmas plan. Write a list of dishes that will be cooked and what ingredients will need to be bought. Write a Christmas list. Make a stocking calendar and fill with little presents.

2
Start your Christmas shopping! Buy drinks, wrapping paper, string, and lacquer. Buy some good hard cheeses and ingredients for baking, homemade mustard, and other ingredients with a long shelf life.

3
Flavor the Christmas schnapps. Bake something tasty and snuggle up to winter.

4
Ready the gingerbread dough. Bake some Swedish Mandelmusslor cookies and other dry cookies.

5
Make mustard and pickled vegetables that have a long shelf life.

6
Bake black rye bread and Christmas beer bread to freeze. Plan a lovely glöggfest for a few friends or many.

7
Bring out beautiful paper and bookmarks and make lovely homemade Christmas cards. Take the opportunity to fold some lovely paper hearts and stars for the Christmas tree as well.

8
Buy nuts, mulled wine, Julmust and other things that have a shelf life that can last up to Christmas.

9
ANNA DAY

Time to put the lutfisk [dried cod soaked in a lye solution] to soak. Bake a really creative gingerbread house and adorn all the windows with Christmas decorations.

10
NOBEL DAY

Make meatballs to freeze, but save some to eat for dinner while enjoying the Nobel Prize celebrations on TV.

11
Try on Lucia robes and check the Lucia crown, the gnome caps, and the star boy cones.

12
Bake the saffron buns first and then use some of the gingerbread dough for gingerbread cookies.

13
SAINT LUCIA'S DAY

Celebrate Saint Lucia! Take part in a traditional Swedish Lucia celebration. Eat lots of traditional saffron buns!

14
Make Christmas candy and store it in a secret place. Set some aside to give as gifts.

15
Mull a mug of wine and look over the Christmas plan. There's only 9 days left until Christmas! Simplify and prioritize! Hang a Christmas garland and enjoy the scent of Christmas.

16
Make pickled herring and other herring with readymade pickle juice. Bake even more gingerbread cookies! Make some to hang in the Christmas tree.

17

Anyone who wishes to cure their own Christmas ham should do it today. Bake crispbread—it goes quick!

18

A little more Christmas candy is always good to have!

19

Make liver pâté or traditional Swedish *sylta* and an English Christmas cake. Make Swedish Christmas crullers.

20

Make a beautiful lantern and tinker with any gifts that may be lacking. Make homemade granola. And why not make a jar of marmalade while you're at it?

21

Shop for fresh produce in preparation for the holiday. Then make Jansson's Temptation for dinner. Use a bit of the pâté for a tasty lunchtime sandwich.

22

Marinate the Baltic herring and prepare the creamy herring dishes. Cure the salmon. Wrap any last-minute gifts and decorate them as much as you can.

23

Boil or bake the Christmas ham. Prepare cabbage dishes, savory pies, or gratins. Take out everything that's in the freezer. Gratin the crayfish and toast to the entrance of Christmas, preferably with Champagne.

24

CHRISTMAS EVE

Cook some rice porridge or make ris à la Malta. Prepare the salads for the Christmas table. Glaze the ham. Merry Christmas! Have at the Christmas feast. Open the gifts! Shine in the moment. Give hugs!

25

CHRISTMAS DAY

Eat fish or turkey and take the opportunity to lazy about a little.

26

BOXING DAY

Examine all the gifts and be satisfied with throwing together something tasty from the Christmas leftovers.

27

Forget the after-Christmas sales —there's still a bit of ham left to make a good lunch.

28

Childermas—think good thoughts, eat light salads and citrus fruit to make room for New Year's food.

29

Buy food and Champagne for New Year's. Don't forget to buy something alcohol free or make homemade ginger ale.

30

Bake a festive chocolate cake or something else that's decadent. Ready the food for New Year's by cooking whatever can be prepared beforehand.

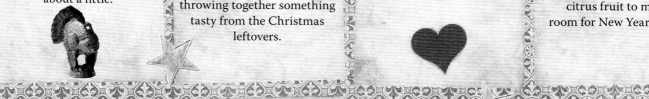

31

NEW YEAR'S EVE

Gorge on shellfish or something else you like. Mix a New Year's punch and look to the future. Happy New Year!

Advent morning

The Sundays of Advent provide a lovely anticipation for Christmas. You want things snug, warm, and a little luxurious —well, something out of the ordinary. Hot drinks with a bit of elegance, the smell of freshly baked bread, and a taste of sweetbread sets the mood when you're about to light the advent candles.

SWED.   DGE

c. raw rice
Tbsp. bu
c. wat
c. m

boil 10   ntil   ilk and
raisins.   ce is t

Advent morning chai

These days, chai is often on the menu at cafés, but sadly they're all too often made from sugary powder mixes. If you make chai at home you can experiment to find your perfect blend of sweetness and spices. Use a Rooibos and you'll have a lovely nightcap as well.

4–6 CUPS

2 tsp cardamom seeds or 4 cardamom pods
1 tbsp freshly grated ginger
1 tsp ground cinnamon or 1 cinnamon stick
10 cloves
3⅓ cups (800 ml) water
approx. 3½ tbsp (50 ml) black tea or 2 bags, e.g., Earl Grey
approx. ½ cup (100 ml) raw sugar
1⅔ cups (400 ml) warm milk

1. Put the cardamom, ginger, cinnamon, and cloves in a pot and pour in the water.

2. Bring the water to a boil, reduce the heat, and let simmer for 10 minutes. Take the pot off the heat and add the tea leaves or tea bags and let it steep for 5 minutes.

3. Strain the tea and sweeten to taste. Heat the milk and froth it with a milk frother or whisk vigorously.

4. Fill two thirds of the cup with tea and the rest with warm, frothy milk.

Warm apple drink

A lovely and fresh warm drink for both the grown-ups and the little ones. The apple drink is also suitable as an alternative to mulled wine, especially for the children.

4–6 CUPS

1 quart (1 liter) fresh apple juice or apple cider
1 orange, juice
1 cinnamon stick
3 cloves
2 star anise
FOR GARNISH:
1 apple, sliced
cinnamon sticks

1. Place all the ingredients of the drink in a pot and simmer over low heat for 10 minutes.

2. Pour into heat resistant glasses or mugs, garnish with apple slices and cinnamon sticks, and serve.

Hot chocolate

Make hot chocolate from your favorite variety of chocolate and top it off with a dollop of whipped cream. The best for a cozy advent morning! If you like, you can spike the hot chocolate with espresso or a dash of rum.

2 CUPS

2 cups (500 ml) milk
½ tsp vanilla extract, or 1 tsp vanilla powder, or ½ vanilla bean
1¾ oz (50 g) dark chocolate
¼ tsp ground cinnamon
2 tbsp raw sugar
⅔ cup (150 ml) whipped cream

1. Heat the milk with the vanilla in a pot. If you're using a vanilla bean, cut it lengthwise, scrape out the seeds, and put them in the milk together with the bean.

2. Chop the chocolate and mix it into the warm milk along with the cinnamon and sugar. Stir. Remove the vanilla pod before serving.

3. Serve the hot chocolate with lightly whipped cream.

Luxurious hot chocolate

Here's an extra powerful variety with lovely dark chocolate. It has a high percentage of cocoa, coconut milk, vanilla, and richer milk. Feel free to experiment by adding a little rum, maybe a little cacao, or lessening the fat and sugar and increasing the vanilla flavor, or simply exchanging the milk for water. Top it off with a little cardamom or garnish with a cinnamon stick.

4–6 CUPS

1 tsp vanilla extract or 1 vanilla bean
3 oz (80 g) dark chocolate (70–80%)
1 quart (1 liter) old-fashioned milk or whole milk
½ cup (100 ml) raw sugar
½ cup (100 ml) coconut milk

1. If you're using a vanilla bean, slice the bean lengthwise. Scrape out the seeds and put it and the bean in a pot together with the rest of the ingredients. Heat slowly until the chocolate has melted.

2. Remove the vanilla bean and serve the hot chocolate with lightly whipped cream.

Danish apple loaf
with cardamom

This loaf tastes almost like a big beautiful apple Danish—stuffed to bursting with apples and cardamom.

2 LENGTHS

0.35 oz (10 g) fresh yeast
¾ cup (200 ml) whole milk or half-and-half
2 eggs
2 tsp (10 ml) granulated sugar
1 lemon, zest
1 tsp crushed cardamom seeds
approx. 3 cups (750 ml) wheat flour
1½–1¾ sticks refrigerated butter (6–7 oz [175–200 g])
FILLING:
2 lbs (1 kg) apples
1 lemon, juice
¾ cup (200 ml) raw sugar
1 tsp crushed cardamom seeds
3½ tbsp (50 g) butter
FOR BRUSHING AND GARNISH:
1 egg
powdered sugar

1. Crumble the yeast into a container.

2. Heat the milk until lukewarm, 98°F (37°C). Pour over the yeast and stir until the yeast dissolves. Mix in all the ingredients for the dough, except the butter. Knead into a smooth dough. Cover and let rise for 1 hour.

3. Peel and cut apples into thin wedges. Coat them in the lemon juice and half of the sugar and cardamom.

4. Place the dough on a flour-covered work surface and roll it out into a large, thin square. Using a cheese grater, grate a layer of cold butter onto half the dough and fold the remaining half on top. Roll the dough out again, grate a new layer of butter onto half the dough, fold again, and repeat the procedure a third time.

5. Cut the dough in half. Put the dough halves on separate baking sheets and roll them into two squares. Line the apples down the middle and top with pats of butter for the filling and the remaining sugar and cardamom. Cut slices in the sides of the dough, toward the line of filling, so you get approximately ½-inch wide strips of dough. Place every other strip of dough to the right, every other to the left over the apple filling, like a braid.

6. Let the lengths rise for 30 minutes. Preheat the oven to 350°F (175°C).

7. Brush the lengths with a whisked egg. Bake them in the lower part of the oven until they're beautifully brown and cooked through. This it takes 35–40 minutes.

8. Let cool and dust with powdered sugar.

Advent bun
with saffron and almond paste

A juicy and generous cake to impress the family.

APPROX. 12 BUNS DISTRIBUTED ACROSS 2 LARGE "CAKES"

0.9 oz (25 g) fresh yeast
⅓ cup (75 g) butter
1 cup (250 ml) whole milk or half-and-half
a pinch (½ g) of saffron (1 envelope)
½ tsp salt
⅓ cup (75 ml) granulated sugar
2½–3 cups (600–700 ml) wheat flour
FILLING:
7 oz (200 g) almond paste
3½ tbsp, (50 g) butter, room temperature
⅓ cup (50 g) roughly chopped almonds
FOR GLAZING:
1 egg
ICING:
⅔ cup (150 ml) powdered sugar
2 tbsp water

1. Crumble the yeast into a container. Melt the butter in a pot over low heat. Add the milk and crumble in the saffron. Heat until the milk is lukewarm, 99°F (37°C).

2. Pour the saffron milk over the yeast and stir until the yeast dissolves. Add salt and sugar and mix thoroughly. Mix in the flour and stir vigorously until the dough is smooth and doesn't stick to the edges of the bowl. Don't hesitate to use the dough hook attachment of a hand mixer. Cover the dough and let rise for 45 minutes.

3. Roughly grate the almond paste for the filling. Mix the grated almond paste with the butter and the chopped almonds.

4. Grease two springform pans. Line the pans with parchment paper.

5. Preheat the oven to 400°F (200°C).

6. Place the risen dough on a floured work surface and knead lightly. Then roll it into a rectangle. Spread the filling evenly on top and then roll the dough into a tube shape starting from the long side. Cut the roll into slices a little over an inch wide. Place them in the cake pans leaving a fair amount of space between each one, cover with a kitchen towel, and let rise for another 30 minutes.

7. Brush the buns with the whisked egg and place the pans in the lower part of the oven. Bake for about 30 minutes.

8. Let the buns cool in the pan for a couple of minutes before detaching the ring and let them cool completely.

9. Whisk together the icing and pour it over the buns with the help of a spoon. Or use an icing bag made from a plastic baggie with a corner snipped off.

ADVENT CALENDAR MADE FROM SOCKS

Got a lot of odd socks in the drawer? Make an advent calendar for the kids.

You need: 24 odd socks, 24 small clothespins, string, felt, scissors, fabric glue.

Cut out numbers from the felt and glue them onto the socks. Hang the socks along the string with clothespins and hide small gifts inside.

Johanna's Christmas

It's that tingly feeling you really want. Like the night before Christmas Eve, when there's rustling in the living room and heavy aromas of spices and frying fats waft from the kitchen. These are aromas you recognize so well, that you've been longing for and associate with magical, precious moments. That tingling sensation might belong to one's childhood, but it never disappears completely.

My lovely, precious moments are like twinkling Christmas tree lights, shining with comfort and magic. Mine are memories of evenings when I was allowed to stay up with my mom to pour the Knäck toffee into molds; of the moment in the kitchen when we tasted the rind of the ham when it was brought from the oven; of early Christmas mornings when the early birds were awake and stirring the rice porridge. The dark of winter outside the windows, candles flickering on the table, the scent of orange and cloves.

My family's Christmas is quite a personal history. Sure we've got homemade meatballs and glazed ham. We make Jansson's Temptation (according to Grandma Alva's traditional recipe) and we pickle herrings and cure salmon, but on our

Christmas table we also always have some Italian charcuterie because we love that. Some years we'll put a risotto Milanese on the table, and instead of ris à la Malta we usually serve clementine sorbet. A Christmas table is like a scrap book of a family's history. For us it features the years when we lived in Italy, Grandma's traditional art of cooking, and my brother's Gothenburg influences.

Each year, there's one additional dish that has to be there, maybe another toffee on the candy table, and a new kooky ornament for the Christmas tree. And yes, some dishes might have to make room for replacements. But the tingly feeling of anticipation? That always remains.

Swedish spice cake
with frosting and dried fruit

This heavenly cake doesn't just complement an advent morning in December but is perfect year round. If there's any left over, you can toast a slice of day-old cake in the toaster or frying pan and serve it with lingonberry cream as a Christmas dessert. With frosting, the cake should be eaten as soon as possible. Without frosting, it'll keep for several days and can also be frozen.

1 CAKE

7 tbsp (100 g) butter, room temperature
1 cup (250 ml) brown sugar
2 eggs
⅔ cup (150 ml) sour cream
1 tbsp ground cinnamon
1 tsp ground cloves
1 tsp ground ginger
1 tsp baking soda
1¼ cups (300 ml) wheat flour
FOR THE PAN:
1 tbsp butter
2–3 tbsp bread crumbs
FROSTING:
1¼ cups (300 ml) powdered sugar
3 tbsp whipping cream
½ cup (100 ml) chopped nuts and dried fruit for garnish

1. Preheat the oven to 350°F (175°C). Butter a loaf pan and dust it with bread crumbs.

2. Combine the butter and sugar into a creamy mixture. Add in one egg at a time. Stir well and add the sour cream. In a separate bowl, combine the spices and baking soda with the flour. Stir the flour mixture into the batter. Pour the batter into the pan.

3. Place the pan in the lower part of the oven and bake for 45 minutes or until a toothpick comes out clean. Let the cake cool a bit before you tip it out of the pan.

4. Mix the powdered sugar and whipping cream into a thick frosting and spread it on top of the cooled cake. Finally sprinkle the nuts and dried fruit on top.

ELEGANT AND SHINY HOT CROSSED BUNS

Brush the freshly baked buns with sugar water: 1 tbsp granulated sugar dissolved in 1 tbsp boiling water. This will make them extra shiny and fancy looking.

English hot crossed buns

Traditionally these spiced, juicy buns are served during Easter in Great Britain, among other places. But the spices and the raisins make them perfectly suited for a cold December morning as well. The icing in this recipe makes the buns a bit sweeter, which makes them that much better, in our opinion. However, the icing can be left off and the buns simply eaten with butter.

30 BUNS

1.75 oz (50 g) yeast
⅔ cup (150 g) butter
1¼ cups (300 ml) whole milk or half-and-half
2 eggs
½ cup (100 ml) granulated sugar
2 tsp ground cardamom
2 tsp ground cinnamon
1 tsp ground nutmeg
½ tsp salt
¾ cup (200 ml) raisins or candied citrus peel
1 lemon, zest
5 cups (1200 ml) wheat flour
ICING:
5 tbsp powdered sugar
1 tbsp whipping cream
1 tsp vanilla sugar

1. Crumble the yeast into a bowl.

2. Melt the butter in a pot over low heat. Add the milk and heat until the mixture becomes lukewarm, 99°F (37°C). Pour the milk over the yeast and stir until the yeast dissolves.

3. Crack the eggs in a small bowl and whisk them lightly. Pour the majority of the egg mixture into the milk, but save a couple of spoonfuls to brush the buns with later.

4. Add sugar, spices, salt, raisins, or citrus peel, and mix well. Pour in the flour and mix vigorously, preferably with the dough hook attachment on a mixer, until the dough is smooth and releases from the bowl. Cover the dough and let it rise for 1 hour.

5. Place the dough on a floured work surface and knead it well. Divide into halves and shape them into two lengths. Cut each length into 15 pieces and shape them into round buns.

6. Preheat the oven to 450°F (225°C). Place the buns close together on a baking sheet lined with parchment paper. Let them rise for 20 minutes.

7. Cut a cross on the top of each bun and brush them with the rest of the whisked egg.

8. Bake the buns in the center of the oven for 12–15 minutes or until they've reached a nice, golden brown color.

9. Mix the powdered sugar, whipping cream, and vanilla sugar and, using either a brush or an icing bag, make a cross of icing on top of the buns when they've cooled a little.

Rice porridge

Rice porridge is a Swedish tradition and a must for many. Leftover porridge can be transformed into ris à la Malta or risalamande (see p. 140).

4 PORTIONS

⅔ cup (150 ml) porridge rice
1 tbsp butter
½ tsp salt
1¼ cups (300 ml) water
2½–3 cups (600–700 ml) whole milk
1 cinnamon stick
sugar to taste
FOR SERVING:
1¾–2 cups (400–500 ml) whole milk
ground cinnamon + roasted almond slivers

1. Combine the rice, butter, and salt in a thick bottomed pot. In a separate pot, bring the water to a boil and pour it over the rice. Simmer on low heat for 10–12 minutes.

2. Meanwhile, in another pot, heat the milk and the cinnamon stick. Pour it into the porridge and let it all simmer for another 40 minutes. Stir with a wooden spoon and make sure the porridge doesn't stick to the bottom of the pot. You can also swap pots halfway through to prevent the porridge from sticking.

3. Season with sugar to taste. Serve the porridge hot or cold with milk, cinnamon, and slivered almonds that have been roasted in a dry frying pan.

Hiram's Christmas

Rice porridge with whipped cream and melted butter. Surely everything was better in the old days—during the time of Hiram, an influential Swedish cookbook author who wasn't afraid to use cream and butter.

6 PORTIONS

1 cup (200 g) uncooked rice
water
½ tsp salt
2–3 tbsp granulated sugar
7 tbsp (100 g) butter
¾–1¼ cups (200–300 ml) whipping cream
FOR GARNISH:
ground cinnamon
granulated sugar

1. Boil the rice in lightly salted and sugared water for half an hour or longer until soft. Dilute with water if needed. Pour off the extra liquid or let it boil off.

2. Add butter and stir until it melts. Whip the cream and stir it gently into the porridge. Don't let the porridge cook anymore because it will lose its puffy, airy creaminess. Just keep it warm.

3. Serve with a cross of cinnamon on the white porridge. And add sugar.

SWEDISH CHRISTMAS PORRIDGE

Overnight cold-leavened country rolls

Light and fluffy rolls. The dough is prepared the evening before the rolls are to be baked.

ABOUT 20 ROLLS

1.75 oz (50 g) fresh yeast
3 cups (700 ml) cold water
2 tbsp high quality Canola oil
1 tsp salt
2 cups (500 ml) sifted rye flour
5–5½ cups (1200–1300 ml) wheat flour (possibly a little more)

1. Crumble the yeast into a bowl. Add the water and oil and whisk until the yeast has dissolved. Add salt and all the flour except for ½ cup (100 ml).

2. Work the dough until smooth. It's going to be quite loose. Cover it with plastic wrap and let stand in the fridge overnight.

3. In the morning, knead the dough on a floured work surface until it is elastic. Shape into roughly 20 rolls, sprinkle the rest of the wheat-flour on the rolls and place them on a tray, greased or covered in parchment paper. Let rise underneath a kitchen towel for about 1 hour.

4. Preheat the oven to 450°F (225°C) and bake the rolls for 12–14 minutes. Let them cool uncovered on a wire rack. Serve as quickly as possible.

Christmas granola

Crispy and spiced muesli is great to start the day with. Eat it with milk or Greek yogurt, with berries and fruit, such as kiwi or papaya.

APPROX. 6 ⅓ CUPS (1 ½ LITERS)

½ cup (100 ml) sweet almond
½ cup (100 ml) pecans
3⅓ cups (800 ml) oat flakes
½ cup (100 ml) pumpkin seeds
½ cup (100 ml) coconut flakes
1 tbsp ground cinnamon
½ tbsp ground ginger
2 tbsp raw sugar
⅔ cup (150 ml) freshly pressed apple juice
3½ tbsp (50 ml) sunflower oil
½ cup (100 ml) dried cranberries

1. Preheat the oven to 350°F (175°C).

2. Coarsely chop the almonds and pecans and mix them with the oats, pumpkin seeds, coconut flakes, cinnamon, and ginger in a large container. Add sugar and stir.

3. Combine the apple juice and sunflower oil and pour it into the container. Use your hands to mix everything thoroughly and distribute the liquid evenly.

4. Spread the mix across a baking sheet lined with parchment paper and roast in the oven for 25–30 minutes. Stir every now and then so the granola doesn't burn.

5. Let the granola cool before mixing in dried cranberries and pour into an airtight glass jar.

Give a tasty *Christmas* present

GIVE THE GIFT OF LUXURIOUS GRANOLA

You need: Granola, mason jar, scissors, String, and a lovely tag.

Chop up 3 ½ oz (100 g) dark chocolate and mix into the cooled granola. Fill a glass jar and attach a nice tag around the lid.

Glögg party

Winter nights are long and dark and there's plenty of time to be together, arranging a get-together and socializing should be simple. Why not arrange a glögg party? All that's really needed is some glögg (mulled wine), gingerbread, and candles. Or offer some exotic salty snacks. You can even bring out a taste of Christmas and serve some Christmas ham or homemade pâté. Here are recipes for both small and sumptuous parties!

You can find many decorative candle holders in the kitchen cupboard. A thick candle will look beautiful in grandma's Bundt pan, and the heart shaped candles will twinkle to great effect on an old pancake griddle.

Roasted Spanish almonds

The simplest accompaniments to alcoholic beverages can sometimes be the absolute tastiest. As delicious with mulled wine as with a glass of ice cold white wine.

ABOUT 2 CUPS (500 ML)

2 cups (300 g) almonds (preferably Marcona almonds!)
6–8 tbsp salt
water

1. Preheat the oven to 400°F (200°C).

2. Place the almonds in a bowl and cover them with water. Add salt and stir. Let stand for 10 minutes.

3. Strain the water through a colander. Distribute the almonds on a baking sheetsheet lined with parchment paper. Roast for 10–15 minutes in the oven.

4. Let cool completely before putting the almonds into an airtight jar.

Christmas nuts

With an exciting seasoning, the nuts that are hiding in the back of the pantry will become the perfect snacks to serve with drinks. They're tastiest when they're still a bit warm.

APPROX. 1 CUP (250 ML)

5½ oz (150 g) nuts, e.g., walnuts and pecans
1 tsp salt
½ tsp ground ginger
½ tsp curry powder
¼ tsp cayenne pepper
2 tbsp granulated sugar
2 tbsp olive oil

1. Preheat the oven to 400°F (200°C).

2. Combine the nuts with the salt, spices, sugar, and olive oil and distribute them evenly on a baking sheet lined with parchment paper. Roast the nuts for 10 minutes in the oven.

3. Let cool completely before you put the nuts in an airtight jar.

Spiced nuts

In the Swedish Westmanlandian tradition of Christmas celebrations these nuts are a permanent fixture. Sweet, salty, crispy, and utterly irresistible.

APPROX. 3 CUPS (750 ML)

3 cups (750 ml) nuts, e.g., almonds, hazelnuts, pistachios, walnuts, and/or cashews
⅔ cup (150 ml) granulated sugar
1 tsp salt
1 tbsp ground cinnamon
½ tsp ground ginger
1 egg white
1 tbsp water

1. Preheat the oven to 300°F (150°C).

2. Put all the nuts in a container. Add sugar, salt, cinnamon, and ginger and mix evenly with both hands.

3. Whisk the egg white and water until frothy and pour it over the nuts. Mix so that all the nuts are covered.

4. Pour the nuts on a baking sheet lined with parchment paper and spread them out. Place the tray in the oven and roast the nuts for 35 minutes.

5. Let the nuts cool before breaking them into bite sized pieces. Store in an airtight jar.

Phyllo dough triangles

Fill the phyllo dough with tasty cheese and you get a quick and elegant little snack to serve with the mulled wine.

18–20 PIECES

1 egg
5.3 oz (150 g) feta cheese or goat cheese
a few mint leaves
2–3 sheets of phyllo dough
7 tbsp (100 g) butter, melted

1. Preheat the oven to 400°F (200°C).

2. Whisk the egg lightly. Crumble the cheese and mix it into the egg. Chop some mint leaves and drop them into the mix.

3. Cut the phyllo pastry sheets into strips approximately 3 inches (7 cm) wide. Keep the strips under a damp towel until you fold the triangles.

4. Brush each strip with melted butter. Add 1 tbsp cheese filling on one end and fold the other corner up diagonally over the filling. Continue to fold the stuffed pastry into a triangle until the strip runs out (the same way you would fold a flag). Brush the folded pastry with melted butter.

5. Place the phyllo dough pastry on a baking sheet lined with parchment paper and bake until they are golden and crispy, about 10–15 minutes.

Bacon-wrapped dates

An American Christmas classic of dates stuffed with various fillings—different nuts or maybe a bit of cheese. Prunes and a twig of rosemary make a tasty alternative to dates.

12 PIECES

12 dates
12 walnuts or blanched and peeled sweet almonds (see p. 57)
12 slices of bacon

1. Preheat the oven to 475°F (250°C).

2. Make an incision in each date and remove the pit. Place a nut inside instead. Wrap bacon around the date and fasten with a toothpick.

3. Place all the dates in an ovenproof pan and let stand in the oven for 10 minutes. Let the dates cool a bit before serving.

Gingerbread nut cookies

Small and lovely ginger cookie snacks in no time. Use readymade dough or the homemade gingerbread dough on page 68.

30–40 PIECES

approx. 7 oz (200 g) gingerbread dough
5⅓ oz (150 g) blanched and peeled almonds (see p. 57)

1. Preheat the oven to 400°F (200°C).

2. Roll the gingerbread dough into small balls and place them on a tray with parchment paper. Place an almond in each dough ball and bake in the oven for about 8 minutes.

Endives
with orange, goat cheese, and almond

Endive leaves are delectably fresh and bitter. The flavor contrasts nicely with all the salty and fatty ingredients of Christmas.

20 PIECES

4½ oz (125 g) almond flakes
2 oranges
2–3 endives
4½ oz (125 g) chèvre or other creamy goat cheese
salt
DRESSING:
½ tbsp white wine vinegar
2 tbsp olive oil
½ tsp salt

1. Roast the almonds in a dry frying pan. Set aside. Mix the ingredients for the dressing. Set aside.

2. Peel and fillet the oranges (see p. 146).

3. Pluck and split the endive leaves. Choose the 20 biggest and prettiest leaves and arrange them on a serving platter.

4. Garnish with the orange slices, crumble the chèvre on top, sprinkle with the almonds, and then finally drizzle with the dressing.

5. For added effect, make a small salad of the leftover endive leaves by cutting them into thin strips and arranging them in the middle of the platter.

Gingerbread sandwiches

Gingerbread cookies and a flavorful cheese can never go wrong. As shown in the photograph here, arrange a tasty bleu cheese, roasted and salted nuts, finely cut figs or pears, and sprigs of arugula or garden cress on gingerbread cookies.

Gingerbread grissini

You can use gingerbread dough to make gingerbread grissini, which pair excellently with flavorful cheese. For instance, prepare the cheese cream on page 35 and serve it in a bowl for dipping with the breadsticks. Roll the gingerbread dough and cut it into long strips. Brush the dough with a bit of whisked egg and sprinkle with some almond flakes. Bake as you would the gingerbread nut cookies on the opposite page.

Warm brie wheel with nuts

A more beautiful element for the glögg party is hard to find, and even the most inexpensive brie wheel tastes decadent when heated in the oven. Can also be served as a dessert.

8–10 PORTIONS

approx. 1 cup (150 g) mixed nuts, e.g., walnuts, pecans, hazelnuts, and/or pistachios
1 brie wheel, not too aged (approx. 17 oz (500 g))
approx. ¼ cup (50 ml) honey
a few sprigs of rosemary
sliced fresh figs

1. Preheat the oven to 400°F (200°C). Roast the nuts in a dry frying pan.

2. Place the brie wheel on a baking sheet lined with parchment paper or in an ovenproof pan and heat in the oven for 15–20 minutes.

3. Warm the honey in a frying pan with a sprig of rosemary to add flavor.

4. Sprinkle the nuts on top of the warm brie wheel. Drizzle with the warmed honey and garnish with rosemary and slices of fresh figs. Serve immediately with bread or tasty crackers.

Fig and port wine marmalade

A tasty homemade marmalade and roasted nuts give the cheese platter a boost. The marmalade is also a perfect party favor for the glögg party.

2 JARS

14 oz (400 g) dried figs
1¼ cups (300 ml) port wine
1 tbsp raw sugar
1 bay leaf
1 lemon, zest
½ cup (100 ml) coarsely chopped walnuts

1. Chop the figs into small pieces. Put them in a pot with everything but the walnuts.

2. Let the mixture come to a boil and then reduce the heat. Let the marmalade simmer covered for about 30 minutes.

3. Put the chopped walnuts into the mixture and pour the marmalade into clean glass jars.

Onion and anchovy pie

Miniature pies make a luxurious accompaniment to drinks, as appetizers or as elements of the buffet table. You'll need a muffin tray or small aluminum pie pans.

12 PIES

1 ¼ cups (300 ml) flour
1 stick (125 g) butter, cold
1 tbsp ice cold water
FILLING:
4 medium sized yellow onions
2 tbsp butter
1 tin of anchovy fillets (3.5 oz / 100 g)
1¼ cups (300 ml) shredded Västerbottens cheese
  (or a well aged cheddar)
3 eggs
1¼ cups (300 ml) whipping cream

1. Quickly mix the flour and butter—preferably with a mixer. Add the water and mix for a short moment. Let the dough rest in the fridge for 30 minutes.

2. Preheat the oven to 450°F (225°C).

3. Roll out the dough. Punch out circles of dough and drape into the pie or muffin pans. Prick the dough with a fork. Pre-bake the pie crust in the middle of the oven for about 10 minutes.

4. Peel and slice the onion. Fry it in butter for a few minutes. Cut the anchovy into pieces. Layer the onions and anchovies in the pie crust. Sprinkle grated cheese on top.

5. Whisk the egg and whipping cream. Pour it on top of the cheese.

6. Bake the pies in the oven for 15–20 minutes or until the custard has set. Let cool a little before serving.

Pissaladière

Onion pizza with anchovies from Southern France. Make your own pizza dough or buy readymade at the store.

10–15 PORTIONS

2 lbs (1 kg) yellow onion
3 garlic cloves
2 tbsp olive oil
2 tbsp Herbes de Provence
4.4 oz (125 g) anchovies
14 oz (400 g) pizza dough
¾ cup (200 ml) high quality black olives
some sprigs of fresh thyme

1. Preheat the oven to 450°F (225°C).

2. Peel the onions and cut them in half. Slice the halves thinly. Peel the garlic cloves and press down with the broad side of a knife.

3. Heat the oil in a large frying pan with high sides. Add the onion and garlic and stir well. Add the Herbes de Provence and let it all simmer covered on low heat for about 30 minutes.

4. Put half of the anchovies into the onion mix. Stir and let them combine with the onion.

5. Roll the dough out thin and place it on a baking sheet lined with floured parchment paper.

6. Spread a thick layer of the onion and anchovy mix on top of the dough. Add the rest of the anchovies and the olives.

7. Bake the pizza in the oven for about 20 minutes. Check that the underside is browned. Let the pizza cool a bit before cutting it into squares. Garnish with fresh thyme. Serve warm.

CHRISTMAS CANDLES WITH DECOUPAGE

Decoupage ('cut out' in French) is an old decorative technique where one uses beautiful paper images. Make Christmas candles to have at home or to give away as gifts, from bookmarks, images out of magazines, or maybe photographs that aren't printed on too-thick paper—yes, everything can be glued with decoupage!

You need: Thick candles of good quality, a photograph or cut out, decoupage glue.

Cut the image so that it fits around the candle. Brush the back of the image with decoupage glue and glue it onto the candle. Brush over the image with a few layers of glue. Let dry.

Adventsljus

Kale chips

Wonderfully crispy chips from the season's pearl among vegetables. Try to do the same thing with the small leaves of Brussels sprouts. Beautiful and tasty at the glögg party or the on the Christmas table.

10–12 PORTIONS

1 bunch of fresh kale (approx. 4 cups / 1 liter)
1–2 tbsp olive oil
¼ tsp sea salt or a pinch of table salt

1. Heat the oven to 400°F (200°C).

2. Wash the kale and cut away the central stalk. Tear the leaves into smaller pieces.

3. Place the leaves on a baking sheet lined with parchment paper. Drizzle with olive oil, sprinkle with the salt, and rub the oil into the kale leaves. Spread the leaves into a single layer on the baking sheet.

4. Place the baking sheet in the oven and let it bake for about 10 minutes until the leaves are crispy.

Brussels sprouts tempura
with anchovy dip

You've never had Brussels sprouts this way before! The batter is perfect for making tempura from other vegetables too—maybe thin slices of zucchini, lightly parboiled broccoli or cauliflower, or sliced onions. Most vegetables become even tastier when dipped in the deep fryer.

4–6 PORTIONS

17 ½ oz (500 g) Brussels sprouts
1 lemon, juice
BATTER:
1½ quarts (1½ liters) oil for frying, e.g., corn, peanut, or Canola oil
¾ cup (200 ml) wheat flour
¾ cup (200 ml) beer or sparkling water
1 pinch of sea salt
freshly ground black pepper
1 egg white
ANCHOVY DIP:
8 finely chopped anchovies
1 small bunch leaf parsley, chopped
1 tbsp capers
1 lemon, juice
¼ tsp chili pepper
3½ tbsp (50 ml) olive oil

1. Combine the ingredients for the dip. Set aside.

2. Peel the outer layer of the Brussels sprouts and boil them in lightly salted water for about 10 minutes. Drain the water and turn the Brussels sprouts in the lemon juice. Drain the sprouts in a colander.

3. Mix the flour and beer or sparkling water into a batter. Add a little salt and pepper. Whisk the egg white until it stiffens and mix into the batter. Add more beer or water if needed. The batter should be slightly thicker than sour cream.

4. Heat the oil in a large pot to 350–400°F (180–200°C) (use a digital kitchen thermometer). Turn the Brussels sprouts around in the batter and then gently place them in the oil with a skimmer spoon. Fry for 1–2 minutes until the Brussels sprouts are golden brown. Place on a paper towel to dry. Add salt just before serving.

Sandwiches
with cheddar, daikon, and radish

If you can get a hold of celery salt, then these simple cheese sandwiches get an extra boost of flavor. Make them as small sandwiches or as open-faced triangular sandwiches.

8–16 SANDWICHES

8 slices of white bread
butter for spreading
a little celery salt (optional)
freshly ground black pepper
5⅓ oz (150 g) aged British cheddar, preferably extra mature
approx. 10 radishes

1. Cut the crusts off the bread and spread butter on top of the slices. Sprinkle a little celery salt on and season with black pepper.

2. Slice the cheese a little on the thick side. Finely slice the red radishes, peel the daikon and slice finely as well.

3. Arrange the cheese, red radish, and daikon. Either place two slices together to form sandwiches, or leave them open faced. Wrap the sandwiches in plastic and press them under a weight for a couple of hours, that way they'll stick together better.

4. Cut the bread diagonally so that you get 8 double or 16 single sandwiches. Serve.

Crostini with Italian liver pâté

Spread homemade liver pâté (see p. 114) on butter-fried baguette slices. Sprinkle finely chopped pistachios on top.

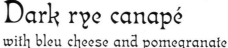

TIRED RADISHES?

If the daikon or the radishes have gone soft, you can put them in cold water overnight—this will bring back their resilience.

Dark rye canapé
with bleu cheese and pomegranate

By mixing cheese with whipping cream and then whisking the cream, you can create a fluffy cream cheese.

8 CANAPÉS

8 slices of dark rye bread, or Danish or Finnish rye bread butter for spreading
BLEU CHEESE CREAM:
5 oz (140 g) bleu cheese
¾ cup (200 ml) whipping cream
1 pomegranate
8 small lettuce leaves (optional)

1. Cut the bread into circles (with either a circle cookie cutter or by using an upside down glass). Spread the butter on top.

2. Tear or crumble the bleu cheese finely into the cream. Whisk the cream until it becomes fluffy, but not grainy. Let stand in the fridge for a moment.

3. Divide the pomegranate into four slices and remove the seeds (see how to do this without spraying juice over the entire kitchen on p. 118).

4. Add a dollop of the cream cheese on each canapé. Top it off with the pomegranate seeds. If you like, garnish with small lettuce leaves. Serve.

Sausage sandwich with horseradish

Swedish onion sausage or a different tangy sausage topping on a sandwich is just soooo tasty!

4 PORTIONS

4 slices of rye or wort bread
butter for spreading
2 gherkins or ½ a regular cucumber
12–16 slices of onion sausage
a little freshly grated horseradish (optional)

1. Cut the bread slices down the middle so you get 8 long slices. Butter them. Slice the cucumber lengthwise.

2. Add sausage and cucumber on half of the bread slices, and if you like, sprinkle some horseradish on top. Assemble with the rest of the bread.

THIRSTY !

Merry Christmas

The drinks that belong in December up until Christmas are lovely—some warming and sweet, others refreshing and chilled: from the classic red mulled wine to modern icy cocktails. Serve refreshing ice water or sparkling water with the flavorful Christmas food, so the palate can get a little rest in between.

"Not-A-Seed" RAISINS

Drinks

Classic mulled wine

This is a flavorful and sweet mulled wine, all according to tradition. Anyone who wants to avoid the gooeyness can reduce the amount of sugar.

8–10 GLASSES

1 bottle (750 ml) red wine (without a distinct character)
¾ cup (200 ml) water
approx. ⅔ cup (150 ml) granulated sugar
1 lemon, juice and peel
1 cinnamon stick
peel of 2 dried oranges
5 cloves
4 cardamom seeds
1 tsp ground ginger
FOR SERVING:
approx. ½ cup (100 ml) blanched and peeled almonds (see p. 57)
approx. ½ cup (100 ml) raisins, preferably yellow

1. Mix everything in a pot and let it simmer (absolutely do not let it boil!) for about 10 minutes.

2. Strain the spices. Serve with almonds and raisins.

Brännvinsglögg

A sharp and strong mulled wine with fresh citrus notes.

8–10 GLASSES

¼ tsp crushed cardamom seeds
2 cinnamon sticks
5 cloves
1 piece of freshly peeled ginger
1 piece of bitter orange peel
1⅓ fl oz (40 ml) vodka
1⅔ cup (400 ml) red wine (without a distinct character)
¼ cup (50 ml) raw sugar
FOR SERVING:
approx. ½ cup (100 ml) blanched and peeled almonds (see p. 57)
approx. ½ cup (100 ml) raisins, preferably yellow

1. Crush the cardamom seeds in a pestle and break the cinnamon sticks into pieces. Put the cardamom, cinnamon, cloves, ginger, and bitter orange peel in a glass jar with a lid and pour the vodka on top. Let the jar stand overnight so that the spices absorb completely.

2. Strain the spices.

3. Mix the vodka, wine, and sugar. Heat the mulled wine and serve with almonds and raisins.

Berry glögg

A nuanced mulled wine that will taste best with homemade or artisan-produced juice with no additives.

APPROX. 1 QUART (1 LITER)

½ cup (100 ml) honey
1 cinnamon stick
5 cloves
1 piece of dried bitter orange peel
¾ cup (200 ml) undiluted blackberry juice or other really tasty berry juice, or ¾ cup (200 ml) blackberry liquor or other berry liquor
1 bottle (750 ml) medium-bodied red wine
¾ cup (200 ml) half dry sherry
FOR SERVING:
raisins
blanched and peeled almonds (see p. 57)
gingerbread cookies

1. Heat the honey, cinnamon, cloves, bitter orange peel, and juice (or liquor) in a pot so that the honey dissolves. Remove from heat and let stand for 3–4 hours so the flavors mix.

2. Strain the spices.

3. Pour the wine and sherry into the mulled juice and heat without boiling. The alcohol will evaporate if the mixture reaches the boiling point.

4. Serve with raisins, almonds, and gingerbread.

Hot wine

Warm, spicy, and sweet wine, or simply French mulled wine.

6 GLASSES

1 bottle (750 ml) French red wine
⅔ cup (150 ml) raw sugar
1 bay leaf
¼ tsp grated nutmeg

1. Mix all the ingredients in a pot and heat without allowing the wine to boil.

⊷ Glögg ⊶

Mulled wine, or glögg, as it is called in the Nordic countries, has a long history. Even in Roman days wine was heated up with additional spices, and in many centuries it was common to serve wine seasoned with pepper, nutmeg, cloves, and more, both in Scandinavia and in large parts of Europe. Today in Sweden, we have a tradition of drinking mulled wine from the first of advent until the twentieth day.

It's still tastier if you can make your own mulled wine. Though mulled wine may seem like a delicacy only to be found in Christmas markets and on trips abroad, it's simple to make your own mulled wine, and you can easily modify the recipes at home. Other than having a full bodied, red wine flavor and being sweet there isn't much restriction to how glögg should taste. Experiment with different seasonings. You can base the mulled wine on red wine, Madeira, or Port wine. Other than almonds and raisins it can be updated with fresh apple, nuts, and citrus fruits.

A fairly new practice is to serve gingerbread cookies with bleu cheese—for example Gorgonzola, Roquefort, Stilton, or Danish bleu—to accompany the mulled wine. Mulled wine also goes well with dark chocolate and dried fruit.

CRANBERRY HEART

A decorative heart to adorn a table or hang in a window.

You need: Fresh cranberries, steel wire, wire cutters.

Thread the cranberries onto a piece of steel wire. Shape it into a heart.

Warm vanilla milk

Nothing is as cozy and smooth as warm milk with a scent of vanilla. A heavenly way to start an advent morning.

2 GLASSES

¼ tsp vanilla extract, ¼ vanilla bean, or 2 tsp of vanilla sugar
1⅔ cups (400 ml) milk
1 tbsp raw sugar

If you're using a vanilla bean, slice it along the length. Mix all the ingredients in a pot and heat, but don't allow the milk to boil. Remove the vanilla pod. Froth the milk with a frother or with a whisk.

Warm cranberry drink

In America, the cranberry is the preferred Christmas berry and you can find both fresh and frozen cranberries. The cranberry drink is also really yummy to drink cold. Feel free to dilute with carbonated water.

6–8 GLASSES

1½ quarts (1500 ml) water
¾ cup (200 ml) cranberries
¾ cup (200 ml) granulated sugar
1 orange, juice
1 lemon, juice
6 cloves
1 cinnamon stick

1. Heat the water and cranberries in a large pot. Let simmer for about 30 minutes.

2. Remove from heat and add sugar, orange juice, lemon juice, cloves, and cinnamon stick. Cover and let it sit for 1 hour.

3. Strain the spices. Dilute with water until desired sweetness is achieved and heat the drink. Serve with a cinnamon stick and a slice of orange in each glass.

Eggnog

For the children make the same drink without liqueur and rum and instead flavor with some freshly squeezed orange juice.

4–6 SMALL GLASSES

2 cups (500 ml) whole milk
3 tbsp honey
1 cinnamon stick
a couple of dashes of grated nutmeg
4 egg yolks
2 tbsp Cointreau
3 tbsp rum
orange peel for garnish

1. Heat the milk with the honey, cinnamon, and nutmeg. Remove from heat.

2. Add egg yolks and whisk for 1–2 minutes.

3. Add liquor and rum. Finally, dash a little nutmeg on top and garnish with orange peel.

Egg toddy
with marzipan and Madeira

The soft flavor of the egg yolk combines well with the sweet marzipan and the dry Madeira. It will be a toddy with almond flavor and pleasantly roasted notes.

4 SMALL GLASSES

3½ oz (100 g) marzipan
3 egg yolks
approx. ½ cup (100–120 ml) dry Madeira or Oloroso sherry
1 tbsp granulated sugar
1 tbsp pressed lemon juice

1. Finely grate the marzipan into a bowl and add the yolks. Whisk into an even paste.

2. Add the Madeira or sherry and stir. Add sugar and lemon juice. Pour into small cups or glasses and let stand in the refrigerator for about 30 minutes before serving.

Grapefruit campari

Campari is perfectly married to all the tasty citrus fruits of winter. And if you want to use freshly pressed fruits, a campari drink is absolutely right this time of year.

6 GLASSES

approx. 2¼ lbs (1 kg) grapefruit
½ pomegranate
ice
1¼ cups (300 ml) Campari

1. Cut the grapefruits in half and squeeze.

2. Cut the pomegranate, break it into pieces, and remove the seeds (see how to do this on p. 118).

3. Crush the ice in a mixer.

4. Mix the grapefruit juice and campari. Serve with ice and pomegranate seeds.

Christmas cosmo
in cinnamon frosted glasses

A sparkly red Christmas cosmopolitan with lingonberry juice is the perfect year-round drink.

5 GLASSES

½ cup (100 ml) vodka
½ cup (100 ml) Cointreau
¼ cup (50 ml) pressed lime (2–3 limes)
½–1¼ cup (100–300 ml) lingonberry juice or cranberry juice (depending on how strong a drink you want to have and availability)
FOR GARNISH:
½ sliced lime
3 tbsp granulated sugar
1 tbsp ground cinnamon

1. Rub the rim of the glasses with lime. Combine the sugar and cinnamon on a small plate and dip the moist rims in the sugar mixture. Let dry. Preferably, put the glasses in the freezer a little while before you pour the drink.

2. Shake all ingredients with ice. Serve the cranberry cosmo in the frosted glasses with slices of lime.

POPCORN GARLANDS

You need: Popped popcorn,
needle, thread.

Thread the popcorn onto a long
thread, and you have a nice
garland to decorate the table with.

ICE BALLS

Serve the drink with a snowball-sized ice cube.

You need: Water balloons, water.

Fill the water balloons with water and freeze. Cut off the balloon and place the ice ball in the drink.

BEAUTIFULLY FROSTED RIMS

You need: 1 lemon or lime wedge, approx. ¼ cup (50 ml) granulated sugar and cinnamon, finely chopped mint or cocoa.

Rub the edges of the glasses with the lemon or lime. Pour the sugar—which you might have added flavoring to—onto a plate. Dip the moist rim in the sugar. Let dry.

Ginger drink
ginger ale

Very refreshing and a little strong. Use the ginger ale in mixed drinks or serve it as is with lime and ice.

8–10 GLASSES

7 oz (200 g) fresh ginger
2 cups (500 ml) water
¾ cup (200 ml) granulated sugar
sparkling mineral water
lime wedges
ice

1. Peel the ginger and cut into thin slices.

2. Boil the ginger slices in a pot with water and sugar and let boil for 10 minutes. Stir every now and then. Set the pot aside and let the mixture cool completely.

3. Strain the drink and dilute with mineral water to desired sweetness.

4. Serve with lime and ice.

Horse's neck
from homemade ginger ale

A wonderfully full-bodied and flavorful drink to toast in the Christmas holiday with. Skip the angostura if you don't have any on hand.

4–5 GLASSES

ice
¾ cup (200 ml) brandy or bourbon
2½ cups (600 ml) ginger ale
a splash of angostura bitters, optional
1 piece of lemon peel for each glass

1. Fill the glasses with ice. Pour in brandy, ginger ale, and angostura bitters.

2. Stir and decorate with the lemon peel.

Christmas schnapps in many ways

It's not difficult to make Christmas schnapps. Write down what is included in the schnapps and when you made it, and then you can refine the recipe each year. The liquor will benefit from being stored for a week or so after straining so the flavors mature.

1 BOTTLE

3 cups (750 ml) Brännvin (or vodka)

SPICES:

- 40–50 lightly crushed juniper berries (5–6 days)
- 20–30 sprigs of various mint varieties of choice (1 day)
- 1 dried smoked chili + 1 clove of garlic (1–2 days)
- 3½ tbsp (50 ml) rowan berries (1 week)
- 1 tbsp whole aniseeds (1 day)
- 1 clove of garlic, 2 twigs of dill, 4 black peppercorns (1 day)
- 1 tbsp lightly crushed coriander seeds (1 day)
- 45 white peppercorns and 45 black peppercorns (1 day)
- ¼–½ tsp (1–2 ml) saffron (1 day)
- 2 tbsp black tea leaves (1–2 days)
- 4–5 sprigs of some spice herb, such as parsley, tarragon, lemon verbena, or lemon thyme (5–6 days)
- 3 dill twigs + ½ tsp dill seeds (5–6 days)

1. Mix the liquor with one of the spices (see suggestions above). Let the schnapps sit for the recommended amount of time.

2. Strain the flavoring, preferably through a coffee filter or a cheese cloth.

3. Ideally, store the schnapps for a few weeks.

4. Shake the schnapps just before it is to be consumed so that the oils and liquor mix.

Anyone who wishes to round off the flavor can add a bit of sherry or Madeira in the seasoned schnapps.

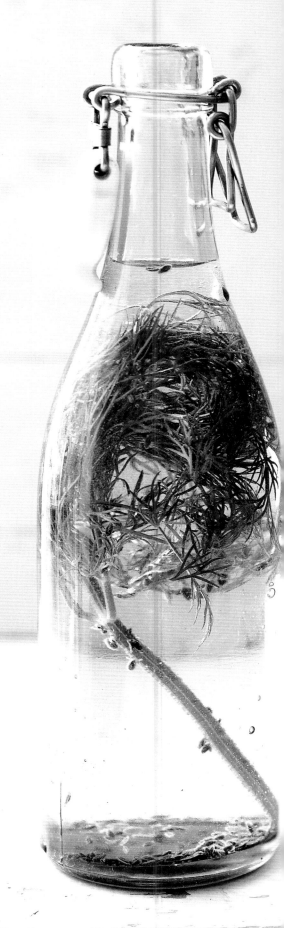

❧ Thirteen schnapps ❧

1. Helan
2. Halvan
3. Tersen
4. Kvarten
5. Kvinten
6. Rivan
7. Rafflan
8. Rännan
9. Smuttan
10. Smuttans unge
11. Femton droppar
12. Lilla Manasse
13. Lilla Manasses bror

** It's an old Swedish tradition to drink these 13 drinks in the listed order.

Christmas Greetings

With a vast selection of Christmas candy you can enjoy tasty sweets all Christmas. Mix homemade candy with store-bought goodies. And why not give away some of what you've produced?

Christmas candy

Toffee

There's no Christmas without toffee so try a new and exciting variety each year. But of course there's also no Christmas without the kind of toffee grandma used to make.

30–35 CANDIES

⅔ cup (150 ml) whipping cream
⅔ cup (150 ml) granulated sugar
⅔ cup (150 ml) Swedish light syrup (or Lyle's Golden Syrup)
1 tbsp butter

1. Place paper wrappers close together on a tray.

2. Pour cream, sugar, and syrup into a pot over medium heat. Let the toffee boil up while stirring with a wooden spoon. Lower the heat a little so that the toffee slowly bubbles a little for 15–20 minutes. The toffee batter is done when it's 248–252°F (120–122°C) depending on how hard you want your toffee to be (take the temperature with a digital kitchen thermometer or candy thermometer) or until it passes a "soft ball" test.

3. Remove the pot from the heat, add butter, and stir.

4. Pour the toffee batter, about a quarter at a time, into a quart jug with a spout or a small pitcher that can withstand the heat. Fill the 'wrappers with toffee batter and let the toffee cool.

5. Place the toffee in an airtight container when it's cooled completely and store in a cool place.

FIRM

TOFFEE WRAPPERS

Butter the tray with a tablespoon of butter before placing the paper wrappers on it and they won't tip over as easily.

Chocolate toffee

Mix the toffee batter with 2 tablespoons of cocoa powder.

Licorice toffee

Crush 8 licorice drops and mix them into a finished batch of chocolate toffee. Top with additional crushed licorice.

Candy cane toffee

Drop 1 teaspoon peppermint into the finished toffee batter. Sprinkle 10 crushed candy canes over the finished toffee before it hardens.

Almond toffee

Mix 1 ¾ ounces (50 g) of blanched, peeled, and preferably roasted almonds into the finished toffee batter or sprinkle the almonds on top of the toffee in the wrappers before it solidifies. You can certainly exchange the almonds for pistachios, hazelnuts, walnuts, or even roasted sunflower seeds.

Lime and pistachio toffee

Grate the peel from 1 lime and mix it into the finished toffee batter. Also add 1 ¾ ounces (50 g) of unsalted and preferably roasted pistachios or sprinkle the nuts on top of the toffee in the wrappers before it solidifies.

Grandma Alva's toffee

Johanna's grandmother Alva made toffee that was a little more porous than the classic version. She made it that way by stirring 3–4 tablespoons of breadcrumbs mixed with ¼ of a teaspoon of baking soda into the finished toffee batter.

Toffee cones

Follow any of the recipes and cook the toffee paste until it's 252°F (122°C) (take the temperature with a digital kitchen thermometer or candy thermometer). Cut strips of parchment paper and make about 15 cones. You can glue them together with a bit of toffee batter. Place the cones in a low wide bowl filled with layer of granulated sugar about 2 inches thick. Pour the toffee batter into the cones and stick clean popsicle or lollipop sticks in the middle. Let cool.

SOFT BALL TEST

Drip a little toffee or caramel batter into a glass of cold water. If the batter can be formed into a stable but soft "bullet," it is ready. Otherwise let it cook for a few more minutes.

THREAD TEST

Drip a little toffee or caramel batter in a glass of cold water. Roll the batter into a ball between two fingers. The batter is ready if it forms threads when you pull your fingers apart.

CARAMEL TEST

Bring out a little of the simmering caramel batter and drizzle it into a glass of cold water. If the batter solidifies after only a moment, it's ready to be taken off the heat and poured into the wrappers.

Soft chocolate caramel

The world's absolute yummiest chocolate caramel.

APPROX. 40 PIECES

¾ cup (200 ml) whipping cream
¾ cup (200 ml) granulated sugar
¾ cup (200 ml) Swedish light syrup (or Lyle's Golden Syrup)
7 tbsp (100 g) butter
4 tbsp cocoa (preferably of good quality)

1. Line a pan, about 8 x 12 inches (20 x 30 cm), with parchment paper.

2. Mix cream, sugar, syrup, butter, and cocoa in a pot. Bring to a boil while stirring. Lower the heat when the caramel batter starts to boil and let it simmer for about 10 minutes or until the paste is 248°F (120°C) (take the temperature with a digital kitchen thermometer or candy thermometer). Stir occasionally. Do the soft ball test (see opposite page).

3. Pour the caramel paste carefully into the pan. Let stand and cool a moment before placing it in the refrigerator. Let it chill for at least 30 minutes, but preferably overnight.

4. Cut the caramel into 1-inch (2 x 2 cm) squares. Wrap in parchment paper and store in a cool place.

Chocolate and espresso caramel with hazelnuts

Add 4 tbsp strong espresso coffee together with the other ingredients and sprinkle ½ cup (100 ml) roasted and chopped hazelnuts over the finished but not yet hardened caramel.

Chocolate and licorice caramel

Mix 1 ½ tbsp licorice powder into the caramel batter. Dip the caramels in melted chocolate and sprinkle a little sea salt on top.

Chocolate and mint caramel

Add a few drops of peppermint oil into the finished caramel paste and stir. Crush 5–10 small candy canes roughly and sprinkle over the finished but not yet hardened caramel.

Chocolate caramel dipped in chocolate

This treat becomes almost like a praline if you dip the cut caramels in 7 oz (200 g) melted dark chocolate. Sprinkle finely chopped nuts, crushed candy cane, or sea salt on the chocolate-dipped caramels. The chocolate can't be too warm when you dip the caramels. Place them on a wire rack to cool and harden for a moment.

Butter caramel

Here, the classic ingredients are made into a really tasty and clean caramel. The recipe can also be used as a foundation recipe for other flavorings.

APPROX. 30 PIECES

3½ tbsp (50 g) salted butter
½ cup (100 ml) raw sugar
¼ tsp salt
⅔ cup (150 ml) whipping cream
¼ cup (50 ml) dark syrup

1. Mix all the ingredients in a thick bottomed pot.

2. Boil the caramel for about 20 minutes while stirring with a wooden spoon or until the temperature is about 248°F (120°C). Be careful that the batter doesn't burn onto the edges. Check with a "soft ball" test (see opposite page) when the critical temperature starts getting closer. Or take the exact temperature with a digital kitchen thermometer or candy thermometer.

3. Pour the caramel into a long pan, about 8 x 12 inches (20 x 30 cm), lined with parchment paper. Let cool until the caramel hardens completely.

4. Cut the caramel into pieces and wrap them in parchment paper or some other lovely paper. Store in a cool place.

Lemon or lime caramel

This is one of Jens' favorites. The soft, pleasant caramel is balanced nicely by the cool citrus flavor.

APPROX. 30 PIECES

¾ cup (200 ml) whipping cream
1⅔ cup (400 ml) raw sugar
½ cup (100 ml) Swedish light syrup (or Lyle's Golden Syrup)
1 lemon or 2 limes, zest and juice
1 tbsp butter

1. Mix the cream, sugar, syrup, citrus juice, and citrus zest in a heavy bottomed pot.

2. Simmer the batter uncovered for about 20 minutes or until the temperature is about 248°F (120°C) (take the temperature with a digital kitchen thermometer). Stir with a wooden spoon. Be careful that the batter doesn't burn onto the edges. Check the consistency with a "soft ball" test.

3. Remove the pot from the heat and stir in the butter. Pour the caramel into a long pan, about 8 x 12 inches (20 x 30 cm), lined with parchment paper. Let cool until the caramel hardens completely.

4. Cut the caramel into pieces with a sharp knife. Wrap in parchment paper or some other nice paper. Store in a cool place.

CHOCOLATE SPOON

You need: Various beautiful silver spoons, melted dark chocolate, ground cardamom, cellophane, pretty string.

Do you have some melted chocolate left over after making your Christmas candy? Use it to make stocking stuffers and party favors. Drizzle the melted chocolate into the spoon and sprinkle ground cardamom on top. Let the chocolate harden before you wrap the spoons in cellophane. Tie with some decorative string.

Cream fudge

Perfectly crunchy and insanely sweet fudge.

APPROX. 40 PIECES

2 cups (500 ml) granulated sugar
1⅔ cups (400 ml) whipping cream
¼ cup (50 ml) Lyle's Golden Syrup
½ tsp salt
½ tsp vanilla extract or ½ tsp real vanilla powder
½ cup (100 ml) chopped pecans

1. Line a pan, about 8 x 12 inches (20 x 30 cm), with parchment paper. (A loaf pan will also work.)

2. Mix all ingredients in a thick bottomed pot. Bring to a boil over low heat while stirring until all sugar has dissolved. Use a damp brush to brush around the edges of the pot and remove any remaining sugar crystals. Stop stirring the fudge and let it boil for about 40 minutes or until the temperature of the fudge is 240°F (115°C) (measure with a digital kitchen thermometer or candy thermometer) and can pass a thread test (see p. 52). Remove the pot from the heat and let cool for about 5 minutes.

3. Stir well with a wooden spoon or a hand mixer for 5 minutes or until the fudge begins to thicken and becomes dull and matte. Mix in the nuts. Pour the fudge into the pan and smooth the surface. Let cool at room temperature. Store in an airtight container.

Valrhona fudge

A stunning and rich fudge with a heavenly chocolate flavor. Its texture is close to that of a truffle. Tasty even if it's made with a different dark chocolate (70%).

APPROX. 40 PIECES

¾ cup (200 ml) whipping cream
½ cup (100 ml) Swedish light syrup or Lyle's Golden Syrup
1¼ cups (300 ml) granulated sugar
7 tbsp (100 g) butter
7 oz (200 g) dark Valrhona chocolate (70%) or a high quality dark chocolate

1. Line a baking sheet with parchment paper, about 8 x 12 inches (20 x 30 cm), so that it juts over the edge a bit.

2. Mix whipping cream, syrup, sugar, and butter in a thick bottomed pot. Bring to a boil over low heat while stirring until all the sugar has dissolved. Use a damp brush to brush around the edge of the pot and remove any remaining sugar crystals.

3. Boil the fudge until it has a temperature of 248°F (120°C) (use a digital kitchen thermometer or candy thermometer) or it can pass a "soft bullet" test (see p. 52). Remove the pot from the heat. Chop the chocolate into pieces and add to the fudge. Stir with a wooden spoon or mix with an electric mixer for 5 minutes or until the fudge begins to thicken.

4. Pour the fudge into the baking sheet and smooth the surface. Let cool at room temperature. Store in an airtight container.

Fruit roll

This is everything that is Christmassy and delectable all rolled up in dark chocolate. It'll be extra yummy if you make the almond paste yourself (see the recipe adjacent).

3 CHUBBY LITTLE LOAVES

6 candied cherries or maraschino cherries
8 dried plums
1 lump of pickled ginger
½ cup (100 ml) walnuts
1 cup (250 g) almond paste (see adjacent recipe)
1 tbsp dark rum
3½ oz (100 g) dark chocolate
FOR GARNISH:
approx. ¾ cup (100 g) nuts, for example pistachios, whole walnut, almond flakes, and candied cherries

1. Chop the fruit and nuts. Grate the almond paste coarsely into a bowl. Mix in the fruit, nuts, and rum. Stir into a uniform composition.

2. Divide the mixture and shape into three chubby loaves. Place on parchment paper.

3. Melt the chocolate in a microwave or over a water bath (see below). Let the chocolate cool a little and then brush it evenly on top of the loaves. Garnish immediately with nuts and cherries.

BLANCH AND PEEL ALMONDS

Heat 2 cups (500 ml) of water for one bag of almonds in a pot over medium heat. When the water starts to boil remove the pot from the heat. Let stand for a couple of minutes before you drain the water with a colander. Press lightly on the almonds with your thumb and index finger and they'll jump out of their shells. Dry the almonds with paper towels.

MELT CHOCOLATE OVER A WATER BATH OR THE MICROWAVE

Break or chop the chocolate into pieces. Place it in a bowl that can withstand heat or a smaller pot and place it on top of a pot containing boiling water. The steam will heat the bowl, so the water shouldn't reach the bottom of the bowl. Make sure no steam comes into contact with the chocolate or it will become grainy and unattractive.

If you're using the microwave, heat the chocolate in short intervals. Open the door every now and then and stir so the chocolate doesn't burn. Let cool to around 86°F (30°C)—that's the perfect temperature to work with.

DIY almond paste

If you have a mixer you can easily make your own almond paste. Give it as gifts or bake something tasty from the paste—such as the fruit roll.

APPROX. 1 LB (500 G) ALMOND PASTE

7 oz (200 g) blanched and peeled almonds
1 cup (225 ml) granulated sugar
possibly 2–4 tsp cold water

1. In a mixer, grind the almonds into a fine powder.

2. Add sugar and mix well (for 5–7 minutes) until it becomes a smooth and warm paste. Add water if it becomes too dry.

3. Store the almond paste in a cool place, well wrapped in plastic wrap, or give it away wrapped in cellophane.

Pistachio almond paste

This paste is a beautiful shade of green and has lots of pistachio flavor. Exchange the almond paste for this lovely variety next time you decide to bake.

APPROX. 1 LB (500 G) PISTACHIO ALMOND PASTE

⅔ cup (150 ml) unsalted pistachios
½ cup (100 ml) blanched and peeled almonds (see inset to the left)
¾ cup (200 ml) powdered sugar
2–4 tsp cold water

1. Peel the pistachios.

2. In a mixer, grind the almonds into a fine powder. Add powdered sugar and begin with 2 tsp of water.

3. Mix all ingredients until you get a soft paste. Add more water if needed.

Homemade marzipan

Making your own marzipan is a bit time consuming but is not particularly difficult if you have a mixer or a food processor. A nice gift to give to someone with a sweet tooth.

APPROX. 1 LB (500 G) MARZIPAN

7 oz (200 g) blanched and peeled almonds (see p. 57)
2 bitter almonds
1½ cups (350 ml) powdered sugar
1 egg white
a little water if necessary

1. Dry the almonds. Run them in a mixer until they begin to oil or grind them in an almond grinder.

2. Combine the powdered sugar and egg white and work into a smooth dough. Add a little water if the marzipan becomes too dry.

3. Store the marzipan in a plastic bag in the fridge. Let it rest for a day before using it to make marzipan figures and other things.

Orange marzipan

It's easy to season marzipan.

1 SMALL LOAF

1¾ oz (50 g) preserved orange peel
7 oz (200 g) marzipan (see above) or almond paste (see p. 57)
2 tbsp Grand Marnier (orange liqueur)
approx. 3 ½ oz (100 g) dark chocolate for brushing

1. Run the orange peel in a mixer until there's only small pieces left. Stop mixing just before it becomes a smooth paste.

2. Mix the orange peel with the marzipan or almond paste and the liqueur. Mix until it is a solid paste. Let it set in the fridge for 2 hours.

3. Form the marzipan into a small loaf (dust your hands and surface with powdered sugar to make it easier).

4. Melt the chocolate in a water bath (see p. 57) and dip the small loaf in the chocolate or brush the chocolate on top so that it is covered completely. Let cool.

5. Cut into slices and serve with coffee.

Homemade nougat

Make your own nougat and spread it on roasted bread as nutella or use it when you make pralines or bake.

APPROX. 1 LB (500 G) NOUGAT

4½ oz (125 g) hazelnuts (preferably roasted and peeled)
⅔ cup (125 g) powdered sugar
8¾ oz (250 g) milk chocolate

1. Roast the nuts (if they're not already roasted) in a dry frying pan. Don't let them burn. Let the nuts cool.

2. Remove the shells by rubbing the nuts between your hands or in a towel.

3. Grind the nuts in an almond grinder or blend them finely. Mix in the powdered sugar.

4. Melt the milk chocolate in a water bath (see p. 57) or in the microwave. Let the chocolate cool a little and then mix it with the nuts. Store in a jar with a lid.

Wiener nougat

A vintage chocolate praline that is quick to make.

APPROX. 60 PIECES

¾ cup (100 g) almond flakes
4½ oz (125 g) dark chocolate (70 %)
9 oz (250 g) nougat

1. Line a pan, about 8 x 12 inches (20 x 30 cm), with parchment paper.

2. Roast the almond flakes in a dry frying pan. Let cool.

3. Chop or break the chocolate and nougat into smaller pieces. Melt the chocolate and nougat together in a water bath (see p. 57) or in a microwave. Mix well and stir carefully into the roasted almonds.

4. Pour the paste into the pan and let it stand and set for at least 3 hours.

5. Cut the nougat into pieces and store in the fridge.

❊ Marzipan ❊

There's something old-fashioned and almost aristocratic about the ancient tradition of marzipan—both in its sweet flavor and in how it is shaped into beautiful roses and small figurines. And of course this almond goodness belongs to one of the oldest elements of European confectionary.

The origins of marzipan are partly shrouded in mystery. The word probably comes from the Persian "Martaban" which denoted a box for sweets. Possibly the almond paste itself comes from the Perso-Arabic area—the combination of almond, rose water, and sugar has long been common to that part of the world.

During the 1700s, nuns in Issoudun, France, are supposed to have developed the marzipan craft into an art. After the French Revolution, some of the sisters opened a candy store in the town. Their products soon became so renowned that they were sought after by both popes and kings.

The privileged in Sweden knew of marzipan even earlier. Bishop Brask ate marzipan, as did Gustav Vasa. Queen Kristina tried to limit the consumption of marzipan by law, since she wanted to lessen the import of expensive sugar.

In those days marzipan, just like other foods for the upper class, was strongly seasoned—with saffron, lavender, currant, cinnamon, cardamom, etc. It was also common to shape marzipan in special pans. A few such pans have been preserved at the Nordic Museum in Stockholm. It wasn't until the 1800s that marzipan became more widespread—even then in the shape of figures, fruits, and vegetables.

Cardamom truffle

A wonderfully fragrant, tasty, and moderately chewy truffle. Its consistency is fairly loose, and therefore it needs to be dipped in chocolate.

APPROX. 35 PIECES

10½ oz (300 g) high quality milk chocolate
0.9 oz (25 g) butter
¼ cup (50 ml) whipping cream
2 tbsp honey
½ tbsp finely crushed cardamom
½ tsp real vanilla powder or vanilla extract
7 oz (200 g) dark chocolate for dipping
cocoa powder or raw sugar to roll in

1. Chop the milk chocolate finely or run it through a food processor. Put that and the butter—divided into smaller pieces—into a jar.

2. Heat the whipping cream, honey, cardamom, and vanilla in a small, thick bottomed pot. Pour the cream over the chocolate and stir quickly into a smooth cream. Cover with plastic wrap and let cool a moment at room temperature.

3. Dollop spoonfuls of the mixture onto a plate, or fill a pastry bag and squeeze little dollops of the truffle mix. Let it set in the fridge.

4. Cover your hands with cocoa powder and roll the truffles into round balls. Let them stand in room temperature for about 1 hour to solidify.

5. Melt the dark chocolate in a water bath (see p. 57) or in the microwave and let it cool a little. (The temperature difference between the truffle and the dipping chocolate should be about 50°F (10°C), otherwise the fat can float to the surface and create ugly spots.)

6. Dip the truffles in the melted chocolate. Grab a fork to help and let any excess chocolate drain off before placing them on a plate. Let set a bit before rolling the truffles in cocoa or raw sugar.

White chocolate truffle

With a little lime, the sweet white chocolate gets a bit of a zing. A simple and very tasty truffle to stir together and roll into little balls.

APPROX. 20 PIECES

½ cup (100 ml) whipping cream
7 oz (200 g) white chocolate
2 limes, zest
¼ cup (50 ml) powdered sugar

1. Heat the cream in a small pot. Chop the chocolate finely and stir it into the cream together with the lime zest. Pour the chocolate cream into a bowl and let cool. Let stand in the fridge for about 2 hours.

2. Spoon out some of the truffle mix and roll between your hands into smooth balls. Roll the truffle in powdered sugar. Store in refrigerator.

White chocolate truffle with pistachio
Follow the recipe above but roll the truffle in ¼ cups (50 ml) peeled and finely chopped pistachios.

MORE PROFESSIONAL FINISH
To give the truffles a nicer finish
you can strain
the chopped pistachios
through a tea strainer before
rolling the truffles in
the chopped nuts.

Peppermint bark

The combination of dark and white chocolate with a hint of mint is heavenly!

APPROX. 10 CANDY CANES

5½ oz (150 g) dark chocolate (70%)
5⅓ oz (150 g) white chocolate

1. Crush the candy canes in a mortar into light pink crumbs.

2. Melt the dark chocolate in a water bath (see p. 57) or in a microwave. Let cool a little and then spread over parchment paper into a rectangular slab about a tenth of an inch thick.

3. Melt the white chocolate in the same manner and spread it on top of the dark chocolate when it has just about hardened. Sprinkle the candy cane crumbs on top.

4. Let the chocolate harden and then break it into squares.

Candy cane marshmallows

Homemade marshmallows are fluffier and tastier and in this case much more attractive than store-bought ones. Delightfully messy to make and requiring both a mixer and thermometer.

APPROX. 40 MARSHMALLOWS

2½ tbsp gelatin powder + ½ cup (100 ml) cold water
1½ cups (350 ml) granulated sugar
1 cup (250 ml) light corn syrup
¼ tsp salt
¼ cup (50 ml) water
½ tsp peppermint oil
a little red food coloring
1–2 tbsp sunflower oil for the pan
¾ cup (200 ml) powdered sugar

1. Mix the gelatin powder with ½ cup (100 ml) cold water in a mixer.

2. Combine sugar, syrup, salt, and water in a pot. Let it simmer on low heat until the sugar is dissolved.

3. Raise the temperature and boil the mixture without stirring, until the kitchen thermometer shows 266°F (130°C).

4. Run the mixer on the lowest speed and carefully add the sugar mix to the gelatin mix. Increase the speed and run until the mixture is thick and white—this takes about 15 minutes. Add the peppermint oil near the end and stir. Then add the red food coloring and very quickly mix together into a beautifully marbled paste. Don't mix it for too long, otherwise it will turn pink instead of marbling.

5. Brush a loaf pan with sunflower oil and pour in the mixture. Spread it evenly with a dough scraper or the back of a spoon (preferably oil it first). Cover with plastic wrap and let stand overnight. Then cut into pieces of whatever size you like and roll in powdered sugar.

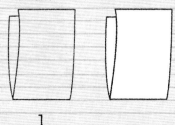

BRAIDED CHRISTMAS HEARTS

Classic Christmas ornaments, which are filled with homemade goodies. You'll need: Paper of two different colors, scissors, glue.

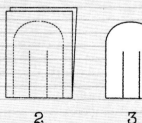

1. Take two colored sheets of paper, about 12 x 4 inches (30 x 10 cm). Fold the sheets in half.

2. Draw a pattern according to the illustration.
3. Cut out the shape and cut along the inner lines.

4

4. Thread the strips alternately through each other. Slide them in one after the other as they fit. Cut one strip to 10 x ½ in (25 x 1.5 cm). Glue it onto the heart like a handle.

1   2   3

OTHER MARSHMALLOW FLAVORS

Add 3 tbsp cocoa powder and 3½ tbsp (50 ml) roasted and chopped hazelnuts and roll the pieces in another ½–¾ cup (100–200 ml) cocoa powder. Or flavor with 2 tbsp licorice powder, or crushed salty licorice. Or why not experiment with cinnamon, cardamom, or dried and mixed blueberries?

Grapefruit candies

These sour candies are easy to make. Just make sure that the syrup doesn't burn—it can happen easily if it gets hotter than 302°F (150°C). The flavor is subtle, but if you prefer a stronger flavor, just add more grapefruit.

15–20 PIECES

10⅔ oz (300 g) granulated sugar (approx. 1½ cup / 333 ml)
⅔ cup (150 ml) water
1 tbsp glucose
2–3 tbsp pressed blood grapefruit
1 tsp white vinegar
1–2 drops of yellow food coloring

1. Stir the granulated sugar, water, glucose, and grapefruit together in a thick bottomed pot. Bring to a boil and add the vinegar. Stick a digital kitchen thermometer or candy thermometer in the pot and simmer over medium heat. Be careful while boiling—the mass of sugar is really hot.

2. Remove the pot from the heat when the thermometer shows 302°F (150°C). Add the food coloring and shake so the color mixes evenly. Let cool for a few minutes.

3. Pour the syrup into Teflon pans, ice cube trays, or toffee wrappers, or pour them into circles on a greased plate or baking pan. Let the caramels set.

4. Break the candies into pieces if they're too big. Wrap them in parchment paper and store in a cool place in an airtight container.

Port wine candies

These candies are lovely and sweet. If you want them even redder, you can add a drop of food coloring.

20–25 CANDIES

17 oz (500 g) granulated sugar (approx. 2½ cups/550 ml)
¾ cup (200 ml) water
2 tbsp red port wine (ruby)
2 tsp white vinegar

1. Combine the sugar, water, and port wine together in a thick bottomed pot. Bring to a boil and add the vinegar.

2. Stick a digital thermometer or candy thermometer in the pot and simmer over medium heat.

3. Remove the pot from the heat when the thermometer shows 302°F (150°C). Let cool for a few minutes.

4. Pour the contents into Teflon pans, ice cube trays, toffee wrappers, or pour them into circles on a greased plate or baking pan. Let the candies harden.

5. Break the candies into pieces if they're too big. Wrap them in parchment paper and store in a cool place in an airtight container.

DON'T BURN YOURSELF!

The candy is boiled at high temperatures. Be careful with the hot contents! Use a flat pan at the back of the stove to avoid accidents.

Few kitchen chores give as much satisfaction as Christmas baking. The kitchen is filled with the scent of cloves and cinnamon. You knead gingerbread and sample a little of the seasoned dough. And when you're done, you can take comfort in the feeling that the pantries are now stocked for Christmas.

Christmas baking

Bake with
the kids !

Gingerbread

Remember that gingerbread dough can be allowed to set in the fridge for a few days. Bring out a piece at a time and bake as many cookies as you need.

APPROX. 200 GINGERBREAD COOKIES

1.7 cup (400 ml) granulated sugar
¾ cup (200 ml) dark syrup
¾ cup (200 ml) water
2¼ sticks (250 g) butter
2 tbsp ground cinnamon
1½ tbsp ground cloves
1½ tbsp ground cardamom
1 tbsp ground ginger
5½ cups (1300 ml) wheat flour + extra flour for rolling
1 tsp baking soda

DAY 1:

1. Combine the sugar, syrup, and water into a pot and bring to a boil. Set the pot to the side.

2. Divide the butter into smaller pieces and put in a bowl. Add all the spices. Add the warm syrup mixture and stir with a wooden spoon so the butter melts and everything gets mixed. Let the mixture cool, but stir every now and then.

3. In a separate bowl, combine the flour and the baking soda and stir using a fork until it is completely mixed. Pour the flour into the bowl with the syrup mixture and mix together into a loose dough. Cover the bowl with plastic wrap and let the dough stand and rise in the fridge until at least the next day.

DAY 2:

1. Preheat the oven to 400°F (200°C).

2. Take a chunk of the dough and roll it lightly on a floured surface or directly onto a baking pan lined with parchment paper. Create gingerbread cookies by using cookie cutters.

3. Put one cookie sheet at a time in the middle of the oven and bake the gingerbread cookies for about 5 minutes. Watch the oven the whole time so they don't burn.

4. Let the gingerbread cookies cool before decorating them with icing.

Icing

By all means, divide the finished icing into several bowls and make several different colors with food coloring.

ABOUT 3/4 CUP (200 ML)

1 egg white
1⅔ cup (7 oz, 400 ml) powdered sugar
½ tsp white vinegar

1. Mix the egg white with powdered sugar and vinegar. Whip into an even, shiny icing—preferably with an electric mixer.

2. Fill a pastry bag with icing and decorate your gingerbread cookies. Let the icing harden completely before moving the cookies into a cookie tin.

HOUSEHOLD DROPS

Sliced gingerbread

Beautifully crispy gingerbread with almonds. Make a double batch and have the gingerbread on hand in the fridge for when you have unexpected company. You can also freeze the dough lengths and then slice them with a cheese grater or mandolin.

30–40 COOKIES

7 tbsp (100 g) butter, room temperature
½ cup (100 ml) granulated sugar
3½ tbsp (50 ml) light corn syrup
½ tsp baking soda
1 tsp ground ginger
1 tsp ground cinnamon
½ tsp ground cloves
approx. 1¼ cups (300 ml) wheat flour
3.5 oz (100 g) blanched and peeled almonds (see p. 57)

DAY 1:

1. Whip butter, sugar, and syrup with a hand mixer into a light and porous batter. (You can also mix all the ingredients except the almonds directly into a food processor and mix in the almonds afterwards.)

2. In a separate bowl, combine the baking soda, spices, and flour and stir with a fork.

3. Chop the almonds.

4. Add the flour mixture and almonds to the batter and stir into a dough.

5. Tip the dough out onto a floured surface and roll it into a sausage shape about 1 inch (2½ cm) thick. Wrap the sausage in plastic wrap and store in the fridge overnight.

DAY 2:

1. Preheat the oven to 350°F (175°C).

2. Slice the gingerbread "sausage" into thin slices with a sharp knife. Place the slices on a baking sheet lined with parchment paper and bake the cookies in the middle of the oven for 10–12 minutes.

Ginger cookies

Wonderfully sticky toffee cookies with a distinct ginger flavor. These cookies can be whipped together quickly.

20–30 COOKIES

7 tbsp (100 g) soft butter
½ cup (100 ml) granulated sugar
2 tbsp Lyle's Golden Syrup
1 cup (250 ml) wheat flour
1 tsp baking soda
1½ tsp ground ginger
¼ tsp salt

1. Preheat the oven to 350°F (175°C).

2. Combine butter, sugar, and syrup in a bowl and mix until creamy.

3. In a separate bowl, combine flour, baking soda, ginger, and salt. Stir with a fork. Pour into the butter mixture and mix into a dough.

4. Divide the dough and roll into two lengths.

5. Place the lengths on a tray with parchment paper and flatten them lightly. Feel free to press with a fork to get a decorative stripy pattern on the lengths.

6. Bake the lengths in the middle of the oven for 12 minutes.

7. Let them cool a little and then slice diagonally. Let the slices cool on the tray before moving them to an airtight container.

GINGERBREAD COOKIES WITH WINDOWS

You need: Small and large cookie cutters, gingerbread dough, hard candies of different colors, a mortar, string.

Use a cookie cutter to cut the gingerbread cookies from the dough on parchment paper. Use a smaller cookie cutter to cut another shape in the middle. Use a mortar to crush hard candies of the preferred color into a fine powder. Put about ½ tbsp of candy powder into the opening. Spread it around carefully.

Bake the gingerbread cookies as normal (see p. 68). Make a little hole at the top of the still warm cookies with the help of a pointy object. Let the cookies cool completely on the tray. Hang them with a string or pretty ribbon.

✳ Gingerbread manger ✳

One of the highlights of Christmas is making gingerbread houses. Ornate, creative, and wonderfully messy! If you feel that the melted sugar is dangerous and troublesome you can arm yourself with a glue gun. And if it's too troublesome to build the cathedral of Milano, you can always construct a small manger.

You need:
cardboard templates for 2 side walls, 1 back wall, 1 roof + 2 short sides and 2 long sides for Jesus' little crib

approx. ½ lb (250 g) gingerbread dough for manger and figures

1 cup (250 ml) granulated sugar (or a glue gun)

approx. ¾ cup (200 ml) icing (see recipe on p. 68)

candy and sprinkles

1 piece of green cloth, a little moss or cotton for the ground

1 star to stick on the roof above the crib

1 small baby Jesus (make a smaller gingerbread man)

3 wise men (made from regular gingerbread men; just cut out a star and then cut in half and attach to their heads)

1 Mary and 1 Joseph (cut out a gingerbread man and a gingerbread woman) additionally, small gingerbread triangles to support your figures, and some animals of choice to graze by the crib, some straw for the crib made from candy laces (available from IKEA) or cotton

1. Preheat the oven to 400°F (200°C).

2. Flour the rolling pin and lightly roll out the dough directly onto parchment paper.

3. Place your cardboard templates on the dough and cut them out with a sharp knife. Place the parts for the crib on one tray and the figures on another. The pieces for the manger may need to be baked a minute or so longer.

4. Bake one tray at a time in the middle of the oven for 5–8 minutes (how much time you need depends on how thinly you have rolled the dough). Be vigilant to keep the cookies from burning.

5. Remove the tray from the oven and immediately place the cardboard templates on the gingerbread once more. Cut off any excess while the cookies are still warm.

6. Let the cookies cool and decorate with icing.

7. Melt the sugar in a frying pan over low heat. Keep all children far away because the sugar gets super hot! Carefully dip the joints that will be attached in the melted sugar and piece together the manger immediately. Let the walls "open" outward and place the back wall with the "pretty" side forward.

8. Use the sugar as glue to attach a small support behind the gingerbread men so they can stand firmly.

9. Arrange the manger and figures for your display.

Maybe add a Christmas tree? This tree is made of an upside-down ice cream cone which has been glazed with green icing and adorned with M&Ms.

Cinnamon hearts

The potato flour and powdered sugar in the dough make these cookies so light and soft that they just melt in your mouth.

APPROX. 60 COOKIES

1⅔ cup (400 ml) wheat flour
½ cup (100 ml) potato flour
¼ tsp salt
7 oz (200 g) butter, cold
½ cup (100 ml) powdered sugar
FOR GARNISH:
4 tbsp granulated sugar
1 tbsp cinnamon

1. Run all the ingredients for the dough in a food processor. Or combine the flour, potato flour, and salt in a bowl. Add the cold butter in small pieces and use your hands to crumble it evenly into a breadcrumb-like consistency. Pinch it together quickly into a dough and work in the powdered sugar until the dough is smooth.

2. Place the dough in a plastic bag and store in the freezer for at least 30 minutes.

3. Preheat the oven to 400°F (200°C).

4. Roll out the dough on a floured surface until it's about ⅛ inch (2 mm) thick.

5. Bake the cookies in the middle of the oven for 6–7 minutes.

6. Combine the sugar and cinnamon and sprinkle over the cookies as soon as they're out of the oven. Let cool.

Cardamom pretzels

Johanna's grandfather's sisters always made these pretzels for Christmas. You make these from the same dough used for cinnamon hearts. They require a lot of tinkering but are dangerously tasty!

APPROX. 60 COOKIES

1 batch of cinnamon heart dough (see recipe to the left)
1 tsp crushed cardamom
¼ cup (50 ml) chopped almonds
¼ cup (50 ml) pearl sugar (available from IKEA)
1 egg white, whisked, for brushing

1. Follow the recipe for cinnamon hearts but add 1 tsp crushed cardamom to the dough. Place the dough in a plastic bag and let stand in the fridge for at least 30 minutes.

2. Preheat the oven to 400°F (200°C).

3. Roll the dough into thin sausages and form into pretzels. Place the pretzels on a baking sheet lined with parchment paper.

4. Combine the almonds and pearl sugar in a bowl. Brush the pretzels with egg white and then dip in the almond and sugar mixture.

5. Bake the pretzels in the middle of the oven for about 10 minutes. Let cool.

Cognac wreaths

Maybe you have a bottle of cognac in the liquor cabinet that you don't know what to do with. Use it to make this tasty cookie classic.

APPROX. 30 COOKIES

2 cups (500 ml) wheat flour
7 oz (200 g) butter
½ cup (100 ml) granulated sugar
2 tbsp cognac
FOR GARNISH:
powdered sugar

1. Run all the ingredients for the dough in a food processor. Or mix flour, butter, and sugar, add cognac, and knead into a smooth dough. Let the dough stand cold for at least 30 minutes.

2. Preheat the oven to 350°F (175°C).

3. Divide the dough into about 30 pieces. Roll each piece into a long sausage shape and fold in the middle. Merge the two ends to form into a round wreath.

4. Place the wreaths on baking sheets lined with parchment paper and bake in the middle of the oven for about 10 minutes.

5. Sift powdered sugar on top of the cookies once they have cooled.

Swedish Mandelmusslor cookies

To make Swedish Mandelmusslor cookies you need fluted tart pans made of metal. These can be found in most kitchen stores. Make sure the oven isn't too cold when the cookies are put in, otherwise they will sink.

APPROX. 35 COOKIES

2 cups (500 ml) wheat flour (10½ oz / 300 g)
⅔ cup (150 ml) granulated sugar
⅔ cup (150 ml) blanched, peeled, and ground almonds (see p. 57)
7 oz (200 g) butter
1 egg yolk
1 egg
FILLING:
1¼ cups (300 ml) thick yogurt
5 oz (150 g) berries
½–¾ cup (100–200 ml) granulated sugar

1. Mix flour, sugar, and almonds in a bowl. Cut the butter into cubes and mix in with your fingers.

2. Add the egg yolk and the egg. Work into a smooth dough. Let the dough stand in the fridge for 1 hour.

3. Preheat the oven to 350°F (175°C).

4. Flour your hands and press the dough into the greased metal pans. Place the pans on a baking tray.

5. Bake the cookies in the middle of the oven for 8–10 minutes. Let them cool a little before removing from the pans. Then let them cool a little longer.

6. Mix the yogurt with the berries and granulated sugar and fill the Mandelmusslor, or fill them with whipped cream topped with jam.

Prostinnorna from Mörrum

A recipe from Johanna's mother's old copy of Hiram's Cookbook dating from 1962, which she has taken the liberty to update. The cookies turn out wonderfully tasty!

APPROX. 35 COOKIES

9¾ oz (275 g) butter, room temperature
⅔ cup (150 ml) granulated sugar
2 egg yolks
1 lemon, zest
2 cups (500 ml) wheat flour
approx. ½ cup (100 ml) raspberry jam
1 whisked egg white for brushing
FOR GARNISH:
¼ cup (50 ml) finely chopped almonds
¼ cup (50 ml) Swedish pearl sugar (available from IKEA)

1. Mix butter and sugar into a creamy batter. Add egg yolks, lemon zest, and flour, and mix into a dough. Let the dough stand in the fridge for about 2 hours.

2. Preheat the oven to 350°F (175°C).

3. Roll the dough on a floured surface, but don't make it too thin—otherwise it will tear easily. Punch out circles with a cookie cutter or the rim of a glass. Add a dab of raspberry jam to the center and fold into a half moon shape. Press the edges together and brush the cookies with egg white. Sprinkle finely chopped almonds and pearl sugar on top.

4. Bake the cookies in the middle of the oven for about 12 minutes or until they gain a nice color.

CHRISTMAS DECORATIONS WITH ICING

You can make the most beautiful Christmas decorations by hand!

You need: 1 batch of icing (see p. 68), bookmarks, cardboard, glue, string/ribbon, pastry bag with a small star-shaped tip. (A tip is a piece of plastic or metal that creates a pretty pattern when the icing is squeezed from the pastry bag.)

Glue the bookmark onto cardboard and then cut the cardboard along the edges of the bookmark. Fill a pastry bag with icing. Squeeze the icing around the edge of the bookmark and let it harden. Attach a string or ribbon to the back with a dab of glue.

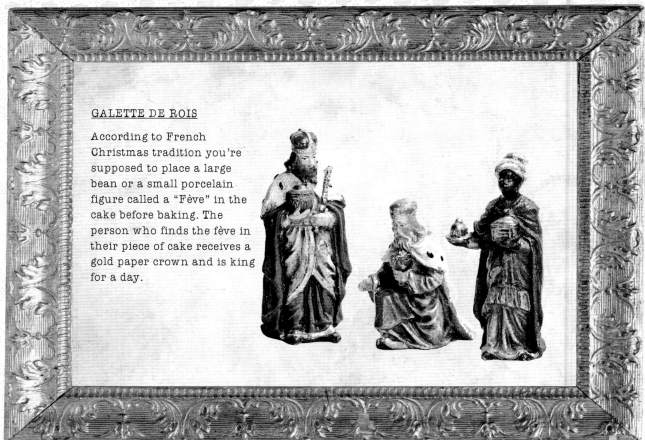

GALETTE DE ROIS

According to French Christmas tradition you're supposed to place a large bean or a small porcelain figure called a "Fève" in the cake before baking. The person who finds the fève in their piece of cake receives a gold paper crown and is king for a day.

Galette des rois
— French king cake

This cake is eaten on Epiphany day in France to celebrate the arrival of the three wise men to Bethlehem and the little baby Jesus.

2 SMALL "CAKES"

2 rolls of puff pastry
3½ oz (100 g) butter, room temperature
1¼ cups (300 ml) almond flour or ground almonds
1¼ cups (300 ml) powdered sugar
2 egg yolks
1 whisked egg white for "gluing"
1 egg yolk + 1 tbsp milk for brushing

1. Preheat the oven to 350°F (180°C).

2. Roll the puff pastry lightly and cut out four circles with a bowl, plate, or the lid of a cookie tin.

3. Whisk the butter, almond flour or ground almonds, powdered sugar, and egg yolks into an smooth and even cream.

4. Place two of the puff pastry circles on a baking sheet lined with parchment paper and use a pastry bag or simply dab the almond cream onto the puff pastry, leaving about half an inch of free space all around. (Push a bean or a small porcelain figure, a fève, into the filling.) Brush the edges with egg white. Place a puff pastry circle on top and pinch the edges together all around.

5. Prick small holes in the "lid" and lightly cut a square pattern using with the help of a knife.

6. Mix the third egg yolk with milk and brush onto the cakes. Push in a couple of blanched and peeled almonds (see p. 57) into the lids of the cakes.

7. Bake the cakes in the oven for about 25 minutes—make sure to watch them carefully near the end so they don't get too dark.

8. Eat the sliced cake either warm or cold.

With pistachios

Exchange half the almond flour for ground pistachios and divide the cream into two parts—one with almonds and one with pistachios. Using a pastry bag, pipe the cream into different layers.

With apple and cinnamon

Cut an apple into thin slices. Turn over in a little sugar and cinnamon and press into the filling before placing the "lid" on top.

English fruitcake
with glazing

A British classic that gets even tastier if it's allowed to stand for a while. In England, it's often served with brandy butter, that is to say, butter that has been whisked with brandy.

APPROX. 16 PIECES

2 cups (450 ml) wheat flour
½ tsp baking powder
20 dried apricots
10 seedless prunes
3½ tbsp (50 ml) pickled ginger
¾ cup (200 ml) walnuts
8¾ oz (250 g) butter, room temperature
⅔ cup (150 ml) granulated sugar
½ cup (100 ml) brown sugar
½ tsp salt
1 tbsp dark rum
4 eggs
FROSTING:
1¼ cups (300 ml) powdered sugar
2 tbsp whipping cream
1 egg white
FOR GARNISH:
nuts and dried fruit

1. Preheat the oven to 300°F (150°C).

2. Shred the apricots, prunes, and ginger. Roughly chop the walnuts. Mix into the flour.

3. Combine the butter, sugar, brown sugar, and salt into a porous mixture. Add rum and eggs one at a time while stirring. Finally, add in the fruit and flour mixture and stir into a heavy and fruity batter.

4. Pour the batter into a greased and floured cake mold that will fit about 2 quarts (2 liters). Bake the cake for about 90 minutes. If it starts getting too dark near the end, cover with foil.

5. Tip the cake onto a cutting board when it's cooled a little. Wrap in plastic wrap. Let the cake stand for two days and it will taste even better.

6. Combine the powdered sugar and cream. Whisk the egg white until frothy and add to the cream. Smooth the icing. Spread the icing on the cake and decorate with nuts and dried fruit.

Lussebuns

Wonderfully juicy lussebuns!

APPROX. 20 BUNS

1.8 oz (50 g) fresh yeast
5.3 oz (150 g) butter
2 cups (500 ml) whole milk
9 oz (250 g) quark or cottage cheese
2 packets saffron threads (1 g)
¾ cup (200 ml) granulated sugar
1 egg
6⅓–7 cups (1500–1700 ml) wheat flour
raisin for garnish
1 egg, whisked

1. Crumble the yeast into a bowl. Melt the butter in a pot over low heat. Pour in the milk and heat it to 99°F (37°C). Pour a bit of milk into the bowl and stir the yeast. Then add the rest of the milk.

2. Mix the quark, saffron, sugar, and egg into the milk mixture. Stir well. Add the flour a little at a time but save some for when it comes time to roll the dough. Knead the dough until it is even and shiny. Let it rise covered under a kitchen towel for about 30 minutes.

3. Sprinkle a little flour on a clean surface and tip out the dough. Divide it into about 20 equal sized pieces.

4. Preheat the oven to 425°F (225°C).

5. Shape the buns into classic "S"s (see picture) or some other shape. Space out the buns on trays lined with parchment paper and let them rise for another 30 minutes.

6. Push some raisins into the buns as shown in the picture and brush the buns with whisked egg. (You can also do this after baking, which gives you extra shiny and beautiful buns.) Bake one tray of buns at a time in the middle of the oven for about 10 minutes.

7. Let the buns cool underneath a kitchen towel.

Saffron swirls

Roll the dough out into a rectangle and fill it with butter and almond paste. Roll it together from the long sides and cut into rolls. Brush with an egg and sprinkle pearl sugar and almond flakes on top.

Smooth saffron buns

Shape the dough into round buns. Brush the freshly baked buns with melted butter and dip them in granulated sugar. If you want to freeze the buns to save for later, it's better to freeze them first and then brush them with butter after they've thawed and are ready to be eaten.

MORE SAFFRON FLAVOR

Get more flavor out of saffron by either crushing it together with a sugar cube in a mortar or by dissolving it in 1 tbsp of cognac before mixing it into the dough.

PRETTY RAISINS

Put the raisins in water for 10-15 minutes before sticking them into the buns and they won't burn as easily

MINI BUNS FOR THE CHRISTMAS TREE

Make cute little lusse buns from leftover saffron dough. Thread a string through the bun and tie it together. Then decorate the tree with the adorable homemade ornament. Do the same with gingerbread men.

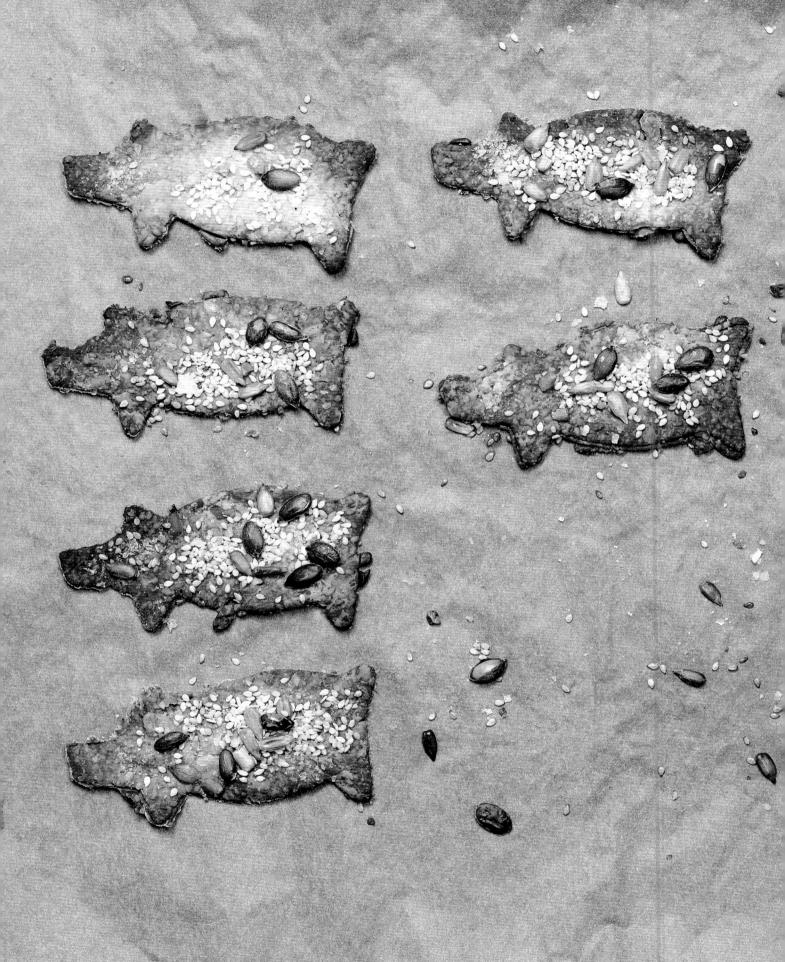

Crispbread

Bread cakes that are rolled thin and fried on the stove. Lovely when freshly made with butter. Remember to wrap them in a kitchen towel when they're done cooking so they stay soft.

APPROX. 20

0.9 oz (25 g) fresh yeast
2.7 oz (75 g) butter
3 cups (700 ml) milk
¼ cup (50 ml) granulated sugar
1 tsp fennel seeds
1 tsp salt
1½ tsp baking soda
1¼ cups (300 ml) sifted rye flour
4¼–5 cups (1000–1200 ml) wheat flour

1. Crumble the yeast into a bowl.

2. Melt the butter, pour in the milk, and let it heat up to 99°F (37°C). Pour a little of the milk over the yeast liquid and stir. Pour in the rest of in the milk. Add sugar, fennel, and salt. Combine thoroughly.

3. Mix the baking soda with the rye and wheat flour and add it to the bowl, but save some flour for kneading. Work the dough until smooth and let it rise under by a kitchen towel for 40 minutes.

4. Place the dough on a floured surface and knead it lightly.

5. Divide the dough into 20 pieces. Roll each piece into a thin cracker.

6. Bake the crackers one at a time in a dry, hot frying pan for about 2 minutes per side. Place them on a kitchen towel and let cool.

Crispy crackers

Eat the crispy crackers as is or with a little butter.

APPROX. 50

½ cup (100 ml) oatmeal
⅔ cup (150 ml) sesame seeds
⅔ cup (150 ml) sunflower seeds
1 cup (250 ml) wheat flour
¾ cup (200 ml) fine rye flour
1 tsp baking soda
1 tsp salt
½ cup (100 ml) sunflower oil
¾ cup (200 ml) water
FOR GARNISH:
2 tbsp sunflower oil
1–2 tbsp sesame seeds
1–2 tbsp sunflower seeds
1–2 tbsp pumpkin seeds
1–2 tsp flaky sea salt

1. Preheat the oven to 400°F (200°C).

2. Mix all the dry ingredients in a bowl. Add oil and water and knead into an even dough.

3. Divide the dough into halves and roll out one piece at a time on a floured surface until they are about ⅛ in (3 mm) thick.

4. Use cookie cutters to cut out heart shapes, piggies, or any other cute shape.

5. Place the crackers on a tray lined with parchment paper. Brush them with oil and sprinkle with sesame seeds, sunflower seeds, pumpkin seeds, and salt.

6. Bake the crackers for 20 minutes. Let cool and store in a jar with a lid.

Christmas crispbread with caraway

Baking crispbread is a little like baking gingerbread—sometimes you have to fail a few times until you get the hang of it.

20–25 SMALL CRISPBREADS

0.9 oz (25 g) fresh yeast
2 cups (500 ml) water
1½ tsp salt
2 tsp whole caraway seeds
0.9 oz (25 g) butter
5 cups (1200 ml) coarse rye flour

1. Crumble the yeast into a bowl. Heat the water to 99°F (37°C), pour it over the yeast and stir until the yeast has dissolved.

2. Add all the other ingredients but save half of the caraway seeds and ½ cup (100 ml) of the flour for kneading. Work the dough well until it feels smooth. Mix in more flour as needed. Watch that the dough doesn't become too hard and rigid. Let the dough rise beneath a kitchen towel for about 30 minutes.

3. Place the dough on a floured surface. Divide it into 20–25 pieces and roll into round balls. Let the buns lie covered by a kitchen towel so that they don't get too dry.

4. Preheat the oven to 475°F (250°C).

5. Use a floured rolling pin to roll the buns into really thin crackers on a well-floured surface. Score the surface with a fork. Carefully lift them onto trays lined with parchment paper.

6. Bake three crispbreads at a time in the middle of the oven for 5–10 minutes, until they take on a nice color. Don't let them burn. Prepare the next batch while the previous is still baking. Let the crispbread cool uncovered on a wire rack. Store in a dry place.

Wort bread

This bread was around as early as the 1800s. It gets its unique flavor from the slightly burnt and sweet wort.

2 LOAVES

2¾ oz (75 g) lard or 3½ oz (100 g) butter
2 cups (500 ml) wort (1 bag dried) or 1 bottle Christmas must (11 fl oz / 330 ml) and 1 bottle stout (11 fl oz cups/330 ml)
1.8 oz (50 g) fresh yeast
¼ cup (50 ml) honey
¼ cup (50 ml) Swedish dark syrup or light molasses
½ tsp ground bitter orange
½ tsp ground cloves
½ tsp ground ginger
¼ cup (50 ml) raisins
7¾ cups (1800 ml) sifted rye flour (2¼ lbs / 1 kg)
butter for brushing

1. Melt the lard or butter in a pot. Pour in the wort or must and stout and heat to 99°, finger warm. Crumble the yeast into a bowl and pour the liquid on top. Add honey, syrup, bitter orange, cloves, ginger, and raisins. Work in the flour and knead into a fairly smooth dough. Let rise for 30 minutes.

2. Work the dough on a floured surface. Divide it in halves and form into long or round loaves. Place them on a greased tray and let rise for another 40 minutes.

3. Preheat the oven to 425°F (225°C). Brush the loaves with a little melted butter and bake in the oven for about 30 minutes. Cover with a kitchen towel and let cool so that the crust becomes soft.

Simple dark rye bread

With baking soda and Swedish filmjölk (available from Whole Foods and specialty stores) you get a really tasty bread without having to let the dough rise.

2 LOAVES

6 cups (1400 ml) sifted rye flour
2 tbsp salt
2 tsp fennel seeds + 1 tsp caraway seeds
4 tsp baking soda
3½ cups (800 ml) Swedish filmjölk (or any type of thick, plain yogurt)
½ cup (100 ml) Swedish dark syrup or light molasses

1. Grease two large rectangular loaf pans.

2. Mix all the dry ingredients in a bowl. Stir in the filmjölk and syrup and distribute the dough into the pans.

3. Place the pans on the lowest rung in a cold oven. Set the oven to 350°F (175°C) and bake for about 1 hour. Tip the loaves onto a wire rack. Cover with a kitchen towel and let cool.

Dark rye bread

Dark rye bread is as traditional as it is tasty. Apart from serving dark rye bread on the Christmas table, this bread is also perfect for more exotic sandwich toppings such as meatballs with beetroot, egg and anchovy, as well as liver pâté and pickles.

2 LOAVES

0.9 oz (25 g) butter
1½ tbsp (25 ml) Swedish dark syrup or light molasses
2 cups (500 ml) water
1.8 oz (50 g) fresh yeast
1 tbsp salt
½ tbsp crushed whole caraway seeds
approx. 6⅓ cups (1500 ml) dark country bread flour

1. Melt the butter in a pot. Add syrup and water and heat to 99°F (37°C). Pour the liquid into a large bowl, crumble in the yeast, and stir until it is dissolved. Add salt and caraway.

2. Work in the flour, but save ½ cup (100 ml) for later. Work the dough thoroughly by hand for 10 minutes. Cover with a kitchen towel and let the dough rise for about 30 minutes.

3. Knead the dough again until it becomes really smooth (use the remaining flour). Form two oblong loaves. Pat them well with your palm; this reduces the risk that the bread will crack.

4. Put the loaves in two greased loaf pans. Cover with a kitchen towel and let rise for 30 minutes.

5. Preheat the oven to 345°F (175°C).

6. Bake the loaves for about 1 hour with a baking sheet placed on top of the pans (so the surface doesn't get over baked).

7. Tip the loaves onto a wire rack and cover with a kitchen towel. Let cool so the crust becomes soft.

Staying up for an evening

In our tradition, the night before Christmas Eve is perhaps the best of the season. All the gifts have (hopefully) been purchased, most of the Christmas food has been prepared in advance, the presents are under the tree, and the stockings are hung by the chimney. Everyone's bellies are fluttering with butterflies, ready for all the tasty things and all the fun the next day will bring . . .

Baked Norway lobster
à la Westman family

In my family, there are some traditions that you just don't tamper with. One is our festive late night on the evening before Christmas Eve, when my brother brings Norway lobster from Gothenburg, which we dine on while sipping Champagne.

4–6 PORTIONS

1–3 Norway lobsters per person
3.5 oz (100 g) butter, room temperature
2 tsp finely chopped fresh sage
1 garlic clove, finely chopped
½ tsp salt
1 lime, zest and juice
FOR SERVING:
tasty white bread
lime wedges

1. Preheat the oven to 525°F (275°C).

2. Split the lobsters lengthwise and place them with the cut side up on a tray.

3. Mix the butter with the sage, garlic, salt, lime zest, and lime juice.

4. Carefully spread the seasoned butter on top of the crayfish. Sprinkle some breadcrumbs (ideally panko breadcrumbs) on top.

5. Gratinate the crayfish in the upper part of the oven for 5 minutes. Serve immediately with bread and lime wedges.

TISSUE PAPER FLOWER

From several sheets—preferably four—of tissue paper, you can easily make delightful paper flowers to adorn gifts or decorate the table. The results can be enhanced if you use decoupage glue to dress cardboard boxes with beautiful tissue paper.

You need: 1 cluster of tissue paper, several layers.

Fold the paper in half. Tear or cut off a thin strip from the folded edge. Then fold the napkin from the short side like a fan. Tie the torn strip around the middle of the folded napkin. Then pull the ends out so you get a circle. Now carefully loosen one layer of tissue paper at a time and pull up and toward the middle. Continue with the next layer and then the next until you have a fluffy paper flower.

Melanzane alla Parmigiana

A big delicious vegetarian gratin that is easy to prepare a day in advance of the day before Christmas Eve. Maybe you have some tasty sausage or pâté in the fridge that you want to sneak a taste of before Christmas?

4–6 PORTIONS

1 large eggplant or 2 small ones
2 tbsp salt to "water down" the eggplant
2 tbsp olive oil (for the entire recipe you'll need approx.
   ½ cup (100 ml))
TOMATO SAUCE:
1 yellow onion
1 tbsp olive oil
2 cans of tomatoes, preferably cherry tomatoes
   (each 14 oz / 400 g)
½ tsp salt
1 tsp granulated sugar
BREAD MASH:
½ cup (100 ml) grated Parmesan cheese
½ cup (100 ml) breadcrumbs, panko or grated white bread
½ tsp salt
approx. 1 tbsp finely chopped parsley
3 tbsp olive oil
ADDITIONAL ACCOMPANIMENTS:
1–2 bags of mozzarella (9 oz, 250 g)
a little extra Parmesan
1 extra tbsp of olive oil for the Parmigiana

1. Slice the eggplant as thinly as you can. Layer the slices in a colander with a little salt between each layer. Place something heavy on top. Let the eggplant stand and drain for at least 1 hour.

2. Make the tomato sauce. Peel and chop the onion finely. Fry it in olive oil until it is transparent. Pour in tomatoes, salt, and sugar and let the sauce simmer for 15–20 minutes.

3. Preheat the oven to 350°F (180°C).

4. Brush the salt from the eggplant slices and arrange them closely on a baking sheet lined with parchment paper. Pour or brush on a little olive oil. Place the baking sheet in the oven for 10 minutes.

5. Mix the grated Parmesan cheese with the breadcrumbs, salt, and finely chopped parsley. Stir. Pour in the olive oil and mix well. Slice the mozzarella thinly.

6. Increase the oven heat to 425°F (225°C).

7. Sprinkle 2–3 tbsp of the bread mixture in the bottom of a pie pan. Pour in 3–4 tbsp of tomato sauce. Add one third of the eggplant slices and mozzarella. Continue to alternate between all the ingredients in the same way. Make sure that everything is covered by the tomato sauce and top it all off with a little extra grated Parmesan and olive oil.

8. Place the pan in the oven and bake for 15–20 minutes. Let cool a little before serving. Serve with salad, bread, and maybe a few tasty pieces of meat and cheeses.

EVEN TASTIER THE DAY AFTER

Melanzane alla Parmigiana is actually even tastier the day after, so prepare it well in advance. Then you only have to heat it in the oven at 300°F (150°C) for 15 minutes.

FUROSHIKI

Wrap your Christmas books
in beautiful cloth following
Japanese tradition
(see description on p. 194).

Sashimi

It's not difficult to make sashimi. The most important thing is that the fish is fresh and clear of color, and that it has a firm consistency and fresh smell. The FDA recommends that fish that is to be eaten as sashimi should be frozen for three days before it is consumed.

4 PORTIONS

3½ oz (100 g) salmon filet
3½ oz (100 g) tuna (environmentally approved albacore or skipjack)
3½ oz (100 g) scallops
1 tsp finely chopped garlic
1 tsp finely grated fresh ginger
2 oz (50 g) whitefish roe or other tasty caviar
FOR SERVING:
lettuce leaves of choice
finely slivered radishes
fresh cucumber, finely sliced or in pieces
soy sauce
gari (pickled ginger)
wasabi

1. Cut the salmon, tuna, and scallops in very thin slices, ⅛–¼ inch (3–4 mm) thick.

2. Mix the garlic and ginger.

3. Arrange the salmon, tuna, scallops, whitefish roe, salad, radishes, and cucumber on a large plate (or on four small plates) and serve with ginger and garlic mixture, soy sauce, gari, and wasabi.

Galbi gui

This Korean dish is actually made from the beef equivalent to pork ribs. But if you can't find beef ribs, just use roast beef, which has a sort of medium tender consistency. The pear will help to tenderize the meat.

6 PORTIONS

2¼ lbs (1 kg) roast beef, or other medium tender cut of beef
6 oyster mushrooms, fried
1 red bell pepper, finely slivered
1 celery stalk, thinly sliced
romaine lettuce leaves
MARINADE:
2 finely chopped scallions
2 tbsp finely chopped garlic
2 tbsp finely chopped fresh ginger
½ Asian pear, grated
¼ cup (50 ml) Japanese soy
½ tsp freshly ground black pepper
2 tsp mirin (Japanese rice wine)
FOR GARNISH:
finely chopped scallion or chives

DAY 1:

1. Cut the beef into six slices, slightly more than 1 inch thick. Pound them lightly with a meat tenderizer (or some other similar tool).

2. Chop the scallions for the marinade enough that the juices are released. Mix the scallion and juice with the rest of the ingredients for the marinade.

3. Combine the meat slices and marinade in heavy duty plastic baggies. Close and store in the fridge overnight.

DAY 2:

1. Thread the meat slices onto skewers and grill them in a grill pan or on an outdoor grill for 2–3 minutes per side (or longer if you prefer your meat well done).

2. Let the meat rest for at least a few minutes before it is served, either as whole pieces or as strips.

3. Sprinkle chopped scallion or chives on top. Serve with rice or noodles, fried mushroom, bell pepper, and lettuce leaves.

PLEATED GIFT DECORATIONS

Use a piece of wrapping paper to make a pleated "flower" for the present.

You need: Wrapping paper, scissors, double sided tape.

Cut a rectangular piece of the wrapping paper. Fold it like an accordion along one of the short sides. Fold the paper in the middle and pinch it together while you unfold the corners. Attach the corners with double sided sticky tape.

ROSETTE

Reuse some pretty photos from magazines or remnants of wrapping paper and make a nice rosette to attach to the presents.

You need: 1 sheet of paper with different colors and patterns on the front and back (it could be a nice picture from a magazine, for example!), double sided tape.

1. Cut the paper into nine strips roughly 1 inch wide: three strips that are about 11 inches long, three that are about 9½ inches, two that are 8 inches, and one that is 3 inches long.

2. Turn each strip so that a loop is formed at each end.

3. Attach the strips with double sided tape. The shortest strip is made into a ring.

4. Tape the strips on top of the other. Begin with the longest and end with the ring.

RIBBON FLOWERS

You need: Wide cloth ribbons, needle and thread.

Cut about a foot of ribbon. Baste a sparse seam along one long side without fastening the thread. Cinch the ribbon and tie the ends of the thread so that the ribbon forms a flower.

In Swedish Christmas celebrations, Christmas Eve is the most ceremonious, magical, and exciting day. This is when we open our Christmas presents and when it's finally time to enjoy the Christmas feast. Be careful to keep the whole day from becoming filled with chores—there has to be time to enjoy the food and company too.

Traditionally, the Christmas feast is eaten in so-called "courses." Herring during the first course, shellfish and cold-cut fish in the second, cured meats and salads in the third, hot dishes during the fourth, and finally desserts, pastries, and cheese during the fifth course.

Christmas Eve

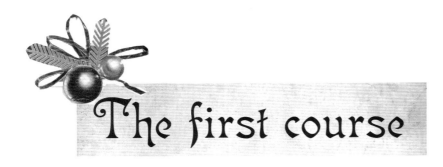

The first course

Classic pickled herring

The classic preserve gets a lovely color if the red onion is boiled with the preserving juice.

8–10 PORTIONS

2 cans of pickling herring (each 14¾ oz / 420 g)
PRESERVING JUICE:
¼ cup (50 ml) white vinegar
½ cup (100 ml) granulated sugar
⅔ cup (150 ml) water
1 red onion, peeled and sliced
1 carrot, peeled and sliced
8 whole allspice berries
1 bay leaf
FOR GARNISH:
1 red onion, sliced

1. Boil all the ingredients for the preserving juice and then let stand to cool.

2. Rinse the herring fillets and let the water drain. Place the whole herring fillets in the cooled preserving juice and let stand for at least twenty-four hours.

3. Before serving, remove out the fillets and cut them into bite-sized pieces, about an inch wide. Garnish with some freshly sliced red onion.

Lemon herring

Exchange the vinegar for lemon juice and add leek and lemon slices instead of onion and carrot. Top with the zest from 1 lemon.

Glazier's herring (glasmästarsill)

This is a real classic that has a slightly crunchier texture than most other types of pickled herring, since the bones are kept in the fish. The bone, however, becomes softer for each day it remains in the preserving juice. This is Jens' extra aromatic version.

8–10 PORTIONS

2 whole salted herrings
2 small red onions and/or 1 small leek
1 carrot
a little more than an inch of fresh horseradish
PRESERVING JUICE:
½ cup (100 ml) white vinegar
½ cup (125 ml) granulated sugar
1 cup (250 ml) water
2 bay leaves
2 tsp whole allspice berries
2 tsp yellow mustard seeds

1. Clean the salted herrings but let the bones remain. Scrape off the skin. Let the herrings soak in generous amounts of cold water for 15–20 hours.

2. Boil all the ingredients for the preserving juice and let cool.

3. Peel and cut the red onion into thin slices, or wash the leek and slice it thinly. Peel the carrot and the horseradish and cut them into slices about 2 mm thick.

4. Drain the herring and cut it into slices 4–5 mm thick.

5. Layer the herring, onion, carrot, and horseradish in a jar or pot. Pour the cold preserving juice in until it's all covered.

6. Let stand for at least 48 hours before serving. The herring keeps for 8–10 days in the fridge.

Onion herring

What kind of onion do you like the best? Yellow onions are the sweetest while shallots are the mildest.

8–10 PORTIONS

2 cans of pickling herring (each 14.8 oz / 420 g)
2 red onions, 2 yellow onions, or 6 shallots
1 bay leaf
10 whole allspice berries
PRESERVING JUICE:
1¼ cups (300 ml) water
¾ cup (200 ml) granulated sugar
⅔ cup (150 ml) white vinegar

1. Boil all the ingredients for the preserving juice and let cool.

2. Rinse the herring fillets and let the water drain. Cut them into half-inch-thick slices.

3. Peel and cut the onion into thin slices.

4. Layer herring, onion, spices, and preserving juice in a pot or jar. Let stand for at least 48 hours before serving. Ideally, serve with finely chopped onion on top.

Herring in dill the Linder way

White pepper and dill is that most Swedish of flavor combinations. Classic herring in dill is given an extra burst of flavor in this dish, as dill seeds have been added to the recipe.

8–10 PORTIONS

1 can of pickling herring (14.8 oz / 420 g)
¾ cup (200 ml) finely chopped dill
PRESERVING JUICE:
5 tbsp white vinegar
⅔ cup (150 ml) water
½ cup (100 ml) granulated sugar
1 tsp dill seeds, lightly crushed in a mortar
1 tsp white peppercorns, lightly crushed in a mortar

1. Boil all the ingredients for the preserving juice. Remove from heat and let cool.

2. Rinse the herring fillets and let them drain. Cut the herring into slices about 1 inch thick (bite sized).

3. Layer herring and dill in a glass jar. Pour the cold preserving juice on top. Let stand for 1–2 days before serving.

Southern Swedish mustard herring

Jens' own take on herring gets it flavor from the lovely spicy brown mustard made in Skane in southern Sweden.

8–10 PORTIONS

2 cans of pickling herring (each 14.8 oz / 420 g)
PRESERVING JUICE:
2 cups (500 ml) water
½ cup (100 ml) white vinegar
¼ cup (50 ml) granulated sugar
MUSTARD SAUCE:
½ cup (100 ml) Skane mustard or other spicy brown mustard
1 tbsp Dijon mustard
1 tbsp granulated sugar
1 tbsp white wine vinegar
½ cup (100 ml) Canola oil
salt
freshly ground white pepper

1. Rinse the herring and let drain.

2. Combine the ingredients for the preserving juice and add the herring. Let stand in fridge for 2 hours.

3. Combine the ingredients for the sauce.

4. Remove the herring fillets and let drain. Cut them into bite sized pieces, about an inch wide. Place the pieces in the sauce. Let stand in fridge for 24 hours before serving.

In the photo you can see cucumber and mustard herring and Cattelin's herring. The recipe for Cattelin's herring can be found on the next spread page.

Cucumber and mustard herring

Jens has been making different variations of this herring for years. Even the herring skeptics tend to like it. It can also be made without cucumber, in which case it becomes a mild mustard herring.

8–10 PORTIONS

2 cans of pickling herring (each 14.8 oz / 420 g)
½ cucumber
PRESERVING JUICE:
2 cups (500 ml) water
½ cup (100 ml) white vinegar
¼ cup (50 ml) granulated sugar
MUSTARD SAUCE:
¾ cup (200 ml) Swedish sweet mustard
2 tbsp French unsweetened mustard
1 tbsp red wine vinegar
1 tbsp lemon juice
2 tbsp granulated sugar
5 tbsp Canola oil
¼ cup (50 ml) chopped dill

1. Rinse the herring and let drain in a colander.

2. Combine all the ingredients for the preserving juice and add the herring. Let stand in fridge for 2–3 hours.

3. Peel and seed the cucumber. Cut into small pieces.

4. Mix the ingredients for the sauce. Add the cucumber and herring pieces to the sauce. Let stand in fridge for 24 hours before serving. The herring will keep for 2–3 days in the fridge.

Cattelin's marinated herring

A classic herring recipe for a wonderfully green and tasty herring. Remember that it must be prepared the day before it is to be eaten (see image on page 100).

6–8 PORTIONS

1⅓ lbs (600 g) herring fillet
PRESERVING JUICE:
¼ cup (50 ml) pure vinegar (24%)
2 cups (500 ml) water
1 tbsp salt
HERB SAUCE:
approx. ¼ cup (50 ml) mayonnaise + 1 tbsp water
¼ cup (50 ml) finely chopped parsley
¼ cup (50 ml) finely chopped dill
¼ cup (50 ml) finely chopped chives
1 garlic clove, finely chopped
freshly ground white pepper

1. Rinse the herring fillets and cut off the dorsal fin.

2. Mix the ingredients for the preserving juice and add the fillets to it. Let stand overnight in the fridge. The fish should be white and solid through and through when it's done.

3. Stir the water into the mayonnaise. Mix in the finely chopped parsley, dill, and chives so that the sauce takes on a slightly greenish color. Add the garlic and season with white pepper.

4. Let the herring drain. Mix it with the sauce just before serving. Taste it—maybe it'll need a little more white pepper.

Vinegar herring

A classic vinegar herring is perfect on the Christmas table, preferably served on buttered crispbread.

4 PORTIONS

1⅓ lbs (600 g) herring fillet
½ tbsp salt
3 tbsp finely chopped dill
breadcrumbs, preferably panko + rye flour for the coating
2 tbsp butter
3 red onions
some dill sprigs for garnish
PRESERVING JUICE:
¼ cup (50 ml) white vinegar
⅔ cup (150 ml) water
½ cup (100 ml) granulated sugar
1 tbsp crushed allspice

1. Place the herring fillets meat side up on the cutting board. Sprinkle salt and chopped dill on top. Fold the fillets down the middle.

2. Mix the breadcrumbs and rye flour. Turn the herrings in the mixture and fry them with butter in a frying pan until they attain a beautifully crispy surface. Let cool.

3. Boil the vinegar, water, sugar, and allspice until the sugar dissolves. Let cool.

4. Peel and cut the red onion into thin slices. Layer cold herring, onion, and dill in a bowl or glass jar. Pour the cold preserving juice on top and place in the fridge. The vinegar herring tastes best if it's allowed to stand for 24 hours before serving. Garnish with some dill sprigs when serving.

Lemon marinated herring
Italian style

One of Johanna's Italian summer favorites is perfect for the Swedish Christmas table. The dish needs to be prepared the day before, but it will keep for at least 1 week in the fridge. The lemon marinated herring is both fresh and tart.

4–6 PORTIONS

10–15 fresh herring filets
1–2 lemons, juice
MARINADE:
½ cup (100 ml) olive oil
1 tbsp finely chopped parsley
¼ tsp freshly ground rose pepper
½ tsp salt

1. Rinse the herring fillets and cut away the dorsal fin.

2. Place the herring fillets in a bowl or deep dish and cover with lemon juice. Let stand 8–10 hours or overnight in the fridge until the meat becomes white.

3. Mix the ingredients for the marinade.

4. Remove the fillets from the lemon juice and place them on a plate. Pour the marinade on top and let stand for 1–2 hours before serving.

Cured salmon
with fennel and lemon

Soft and sweet with a fresh note of lemon and the oh-so-finely sliced fennel.

6–8 PORTIONS

1½ lbs (700 g) salmon fillet, with skin
2 tbsp salt
1½ tbsp granulated sugar
¼ tsp freshly ground white pepper
1 lemon, zest
1 fennel
dill

1. Freeze the salmon for 72 hours. Bring it out to defrost a few hours before it is to be cured.

2. Mix salt and sugar and sprinkle on the salmon. Rub it in lightly. Grind white pepper over the salmon and zest the lemon peel. Cut the fennel as thinly as you can, preferably with a mandolin.

3. Divide the salmon into halves and place them together, meat sides together and the fennel in between. Place in a plastic bag and let rest in the fridge for 24–48 hours.

4. Serve the salmon cut into thin slices with dill, fennel, and preferably a little extra lemon zest on top.

Smoked fish with whitefish roe

Smoked fish has a given place on a Scandinavian Christmas table. Lovely Swedish roe in sour cream is a simple but perfect accompaniment.

6–8 PORTIONS

7 oz (200 g) smoked fish, for example smoked salmon,
   char or rainbow, smoked salmon fins, or smoked lamprey
ROE SAUCE:
3½ oz (100 g) whitefish roe (or other fish roe)
¾ cup (200 ml) sour cream
2 tbsp finely chopped dill

1. Let the roe and sour cream drain for a couple of hours in separate coffee filters in the fridge. This will give the sauce a firm consistency.

2. Combine the roe, sour cream, and dill. Sample. Serve the sauce with the smoked fish.

Kipper salad

If you can find authentic kippers—smoked Baltic herring (not regular herring) that is—this salad will become extra tasty.

6–8 SMALL PORTIONS

2 oranges
7 oz (200 g) green beans, wax beans, or edamame beans
7 oz (200 g) gutted kippers
2 medium boiled eggs, cut into wedges
4 boiled and peeled potatoes, cut into small pieces
1 yellow onion, sliced
12–16 black pitted olives
1 large handful of roughly chopped mixed greens
VINAIGRETTE:
2 tsp red wine vinegar
1 garlic clove, finely chopped
freshly ground black pepper
salt
3 tbsp olive oil

1. With a sharp knife, cut away the peel and the pith of the oranges. Fillet the segments (see p. 146). Cut the meat of the fruit into small pieces.

2. Boil the beans in lightly salted water until they soften but don't let them get mushy. Drain in a colander and let cool.

3. Mix all the ingredients for the vinaigrette.

4. Place all the salad ingredients in a large bowl.

5. Pour in the vinaigrette and mix. Serve in a large bowl or on a serving dish.

Salmon

There are many different recipes for this classic. The salt hardens the fish, while the sugar softens it, so that everyone can experiment their way to their preferred texture. In times past, gravlax was served in thick slices. That can also be tasty. If you like, you can cut away the skin, sliver it, and grill it quickly and serve the skin as edible garnish on the salmon tray.

6–8 PORTIONS

2 ¼ lbs (1 kg) salmon fillet, with skin, divided into halves or in pieces
3–4 tbsp granulated sugar
3 tbsp salt
2 tsp roughly crushed white peppercorns (can be exchanged for black pepper or rose pepper)
½ cup (100 ml) roughly chopped dill (you can even add a few dill seeds)

1. Dry the salmon with kitchen towels. Remove all the bones and fins with a sharp knife and kitchen tweezers or with your fingers. Leave the skin on.

2. Mix the sugar, salt, and pepper and rub the salmon with some of the mixture. Place one piece skin side down in the bottom of a pan. Sprinkle more of the mixture on top and then add the dill. Place the other salmon piece on top, with the skin side up. Sprinkle on the last of the sugar mixture. Let stand for half an hour until that the mixture dissolves.

3. Cover the pan with plastic wrap; you may even want to place a cutting board on top as a weight. Let stand in the fridge for 24–48 hours before serving. Turn the fish after half the time.

4. Drain the juice that's formed. Scrape off the remaining herbs and cut the salmon at an angle into wide, thin slices. Serve with mustard-dill sauce (see recipe adjacent).

Salmon in preserving juice

You can also marinate the salmon in preserving juice. It makes the salmon juicy and soft. Boil 2 cups (500 ml) water, ¼ cup (50 ml) coarse salt, ¼ cup (50 ml) granulated sugar, 1 tbsp coriander seeds, and 1 tsp whole white peppercorns. Let the preserving juice cool. Place 2 ¼ lbs (1 kg) salmon fillet in a tight plastic bag and pour in the cooled juice. Close the bag. Let stand in the fridge for 48 hours before serving. Let the salmon drain in a colander.

Salmon in spirits

Follow the recipe for marinated salmon, but rub the salmon with 1–3 tbsp of cognac, Armagnac, gin, calvados, vodka, or spiced liquor before dill and pepper is added.

Mustard-dill sauce

This classic sauce, also known as Hovmästarsås or Gravlaxsås, is delicious with other marinated fish and with shellfish. Sometimes the dill is eliminated and then the sauce is simply called mustard sauce.

4 PORTIONS

2 tbsp granulated sugar
¼–½ tsp salt
4 tbsp finely chopped dill
3 tbsp Swedish sweet mustard (available at IKEA and online)
possibly 1 tbsp Dijon mustard
1 tbsp red wine vinegar
½ cup (100 ml) Canola oil
salt to taste
freshly ground white pepper

1. Mix the sugar, salt, and dill (it is said that the aroma of the dill comes out best this way). Add the mustard and vinegar.

2. Stir in the oil, a little at a time, so the sauce doesn't crack or break. Add salt and pepper to taste. Let stand a little while before serving.

Mustard-dill sauce à la crème

Regular mustard-dill sauce becomes slightly softer if you add a little cream.

8 SMALL PORTIONS

2 tbsp granulated sugar
¼–½ tsp salt
4 tbsp finely chopped dill
3 tbsp Swedish sweet mustard (available at IKEA and online)
1 tbsp Dijon mustard
1 tbsp red wine vinegar
¼ cup (50 ml) Canola oil
¼ cup (50 ml) whipping cream
salt to taste
freshly ground white pepper

1. Mix sugar, salt, and dill. Stir in the mustard and vinegar.

2. Stir in the oil a little at a time so that the sauce doesn't break. Pour in the cream. Add salt and pepper to taste. Let stand a moment before serving.

Danish style Mustard-dill sauce

Danish variations on this sauce can contain egg yolks, and/or syrup or brown sugar. Some lace the sauce with a little cognac or honey.

Marinated whitefish

Whitefish is ideal when marinated and is perfect for the Christmas table, or as a light supper with delicious crispbread and a cold beer or mumma.

4–6 PORTIONS

2 sides of whitefish fillets
2 tbsp granulated sugar
2 tbsp fine salt
½ tbsp juniper berries
½ tbsp whole rose pepper
1 lemon, zest
dill

1. Begin by removing the bones from the whitefish filets with kitchen tweezers. Then, place the fillets in a pan. Sprinkle sugar and salt on top—half on each side.

2. Crush the juniper berries and rose pepper in a mortar and sprinkle over the fish. Also sprinkle with the lemon zest. Place the fillets together.

3. Let the fish stand in the fridge for 24–48 hours. Cut it thinly and garnish with extra rose pepper and dill if desired.

Mumma

Everyone has their own recipe for this classic Swedish Christmas drink. Some mix with white wine, others add cardamom seeds. Some top it off with Renat Brännvin or gin instead of Madeira. Some add blackcurrant juice. Experiment to find your own preferred mixture!

1 PITCHER, APPROX. 8 GLASSES

1 bottle Porter (22 fl oz / 660 ml)
2 bottles Pilsner (111 fl oz / 330 ml)
1⅓ cup (330 ml) lemonade
½ cup (50 ml) Madeira

1. Combine the porter and pilsner in a chilled pitcher.

2. Add the lemonade and Madeira. Drink at once.

Egg halves to your liking

Egg halves are really tasty and can be made any way you want. Choose between smoked fish, shellfish, caviar, soft cheese, hard cheese, mayonnaise, mustard, and all sorts of things.

8 SMALL PORTIONS

8 organic eggs
FILLING:
* mayonnaise, thick yogurt, or drained sour cream
* Mustard-dill sauce
* Kalles caviar or cheese spread
* mustard or horseradish cream
* whitefish roe, salmon roe, or lump fish roe
* warm smoked salmon or mackerel
* cold smoked salmon
* shrimp or crayfish tails
* herring
* anchovy
* capers
* pickled peppers
* radishes
* cucumber
* finely chopped red onion
* finely chopped dill, parsley, or chives
* dill twigs, parsley sprigs, or chives
* grated cheese
* freshly ground black pepper

1. First boil the eggs. Place them in cold water and once it starts to boil, let them cook for about 4 minutes. Run cold water over the eggs, peel them, and cut them in halves. Place on a serving tray.

2. Fill the egg halves and serve them at once, or cover and put them in the fridge. Decorate with dill sprigs and such just before serving.

Mayonnaise

No mayonnaise is as tasty as the one you make yourself. Remember that the eggs and oil must be at room temperature to make this work. So take them from the fridge ahead of time.

1 BATCH

2 egg yolks
1 tsp vinegar
1 tsp Dijon mustard
1 cup (250 ml) Canola oil
salt and pepper

1. Place the egg yolks in a bowl with a round bottom. Pour in half of the vinegar and the mustard and a little salt and pepper.

2. Add the oil while stirring vigorously, preferably with an electric whisk. Begin drop by drop and then eventually pour it in an even stream.

3. Lastly, add the rest of the vinegar. Season with salt and pepper to taste.

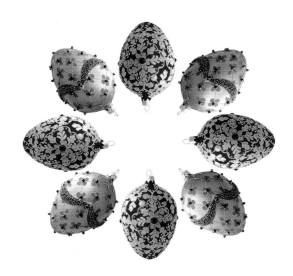

Christmas ham to your liking

You can either boil or bake a Christmas ham. The ham that is baked in the oven is both richer in flavor and firmer in texture, while the boiled ham allows for a tasty stock for dipping, for those who prefer that. At low temperature, the ham becomes somewhat more tender and juicier. How you choose to prepare the ham is really just a matter of preference. A kitchen thermometer is a must for each one of these methods. A round ham requires a longer cooking time than an oblong-shaped ham, and cooking times vary quite a lot from one ham to another. An inner temperature of around 155–160°F (69–71°C) allows for really juicy meat, but if you like that traditional, slightly dry meat you should let the inner temperature rise to 165–167°F (74–75°C).

---

1 cured ham (9–13 lbs / 4–6 kg)
STOCK FOR OPTION C:
4 cloves
1 yellow onion
1 carrot
5 whole allspice berries
2 tbsp Swedish sweet mustard
1 tbsp granulated sugar
1 egg
¾ cup (200 ml) breadcrumbs

1. Soak the ham for 3–6 hours or follow the instructions on the packaging.

2. Preheat the oven to 250°F or 350°F (125°C or 175°C). Remove the ham and dry it well.

3. Prepare the ham in one of the following ways:

A) Bake the ham at a low temperature of 260°F (125°C) for about 4 hours, or until it reaches an inner temperature of 155–167°F (69°75°C).

B) Bake the ham in aluminum foil at 350°F (175°C) for 2–2½ hours or until it reaches an inner temperature of 155–167°F (69–75°C).

C) Place the ham in a pot. Fill with water and bring to a boil, and then pour away the water and the foam. Pour in fresh water—ideally use boiled water from the kettle—until the ham is just covered. Add the spices for the stock and let it simmer with the lid slightly cracked over as low a heat as possible. Simmer for about 3 hours or until it reaches an inner temperature of 155–167°F (69–75°C).

4. Remove the ham from the oven or remove from the boiled stock and set aside for 10 minutes. Save the juices in the aluminum foil or the liquid in the pot. It can be used for dipping into the pot or for kale.

5. Increase the oven temperature to 400°F (200°C). Pull off or cut away the rind from the ham, but leave the fat underneath. Return the ham to the baking tray.

6. Mix the mustard, sugar, and egg and spread the mixture on the top of the ham. Sprinkle with breadcrumbs. Brown for 10–15 minutes until the ham has attained a lovely golden color. Let cool.

Glazing with shine
and the taste of the Mediterranean kitchen

Beautifully shiny ham that has a hint of rosemary. Perfect with both risotto and Italian cheeses if you're looking for an alternative and Italian-inspired Christmas table.

---

1 BATCH

2–3 sprigs of fresh rosemary
3–4 garlic cloves
4 tbsp brown sugar

1. Score grooves in the ham and insert sprigs of rosemary and the peeled garlic cloves into the slits. Sprinkle brown sugar over the whole ham.

2. Preheat the oven to 400°F (200°C). Glaze the ham in the oven for about 20 minutes or until the sugar has melted and the ham has attained a nice color and shine.

Almond browning

Make the ham a little more attractive without making its flavor stand out too much in comparison to the traditional flavors on the Christmas table.

1 BATCH

1 egg yolk
2 tbsp Swedish sweet mustard (available at IKEA or online)
2 tbsp honey
2 oz (50 g) almond flakes

1. Preheat the oven to 400°F (200°C). Stir the egg yolk, mustard, and honey together. Brush the ham with the mixture but save some of it for later. Carefully put the almonds into the remaining mixture and spread it on top of the ham.

2. Glaze the ham in the oven for 15–20 minutes or until it attains a nice color.

Sesame seed browning

Give the ham an Asian feel with the flavors of ginger and sesame seeds. The seeds give the ham a deliciously crispy surface.

1 BATCH

1 egg yolk
2 tbsp Swedish sweet mustard (available at IKEA or online)
2 tbsp honey
1 tbsp grated ginger
¼ cup (50 ml) sesame seeds

1. Preheat the oven to 400°F (200°C). Stir the egg yolk, mustard, honey, and grated ginger together. Brush the ham with the mixture but save some of it. Carefully put the sesame seeds into the remaining mixture and spread it on top of the ham.

2. Glaze the ham in the oven for 15–20 minutes or until it attains a nice color.

Give a tasty *Christmas* present

Creamy mustard

Making mustard is both easy and challenging at the same time. Don't over-season and be sure to let the mustard stand for at least a few days in the fridge so the flavors have time to develop.

1 BATCH

approx. 1 oz (25 g) mustard powder (Colman's)
¼ cup (50 ml) water
¼ cup (50 ml) whipping cream
1½–2 tbsp raw sugar
½–¾ tsp salt
possibly ¼–¾ tsp black pepper, all spice, chili powder, ground cloves, ground mace, ground nutmeg, or finely dried herbs
1 tbsp Canola oil
1–2 tsp vinegar, wine, cognac, vinegar, or lemon juice

1. Mix the mustard powder, water, cream, sugar, salt, and spices in a thick bottomed pan. Boil and let simmer while stirring continuously for 3–4 minutes until the mixture thickens. Watch out, it burns easily and sticks to the bottom!

2. Remove from the heat and whisk for 3–4 minutes. Let cool and put in the fridge overnight.

3. Stir the oil in a little at a time. Sample and possibly add more salt and more of any other flavoring. Mustard keeps for 1 week in the fridge.

Coarse grained mustard

If you like, you can experiment with the same flavors as in the creamy variety.

1 BATCH

¼ cup (50 ml) yellow mustard seeds
5 tsp (25 ml) brown mustard seeds
½ cup (125 ml) water
½ cup (100 ml) raw sugar
½–1 tsp salt
2 tbsp white wine vinegar
2 tbsp Canola oil

1. Boil the mustard seeds, water, and sugar. Mix in a mixer or with an immersion blender. Be careful—the liquid is hot.

2. Add salt and vinegar and stir the oil in a little at a time. Let stand for 48–72 hours.

3. Sample and adjust the flavoring as needed. Let stand for 1 week in the fridge so the flavors can develop.

Italian chicken liver pâté

A spreadable pâté that is served on crostini in Toscana.

ENOUGH FOR MANY SANDWICHES

7 oz (200 g) chicken liver
½–⅔ cups (100–150 ml) red wine
1 bay leaf
1 shallot
1 carrot
1 celery stalk
¼ cup (50 ml) olive oil
2 anchovy fillets
2 tbsp tomato purée
salt and freshly ground black pepper
1 lemon, zest and juice
some sprigs of flat leaf parsley
1 tbsp capers

1. Marinate the chicken liver overnight in the red wine with a bay leaf.

2. Peel the onion and the carrot. Chop the onion finely. Cut the carrot and celery into thin slices. Heat the olive oil in a frying pan. Fry the onion until soft and transparent. Add carrot and celery slices and fry for another couple of minutes. Add anchovy fillets and tomato purée and stir.

3. Remove the chicken liver from the wine and cut into cubes. Place the liver in the pot and fry until well done. Add salt and pepper.

4. Add lemon juice and zest. Chop the parsley finely and add it and the capers to pan. Mix all with an immersion blender into a smooth paste.

.

Jens' Christmas pâté

This creamy pâté is jazzed up with a few anchovies and whole capers. Fry a small sample in the frying pan to determine whether the seasoning needs to be adjusted before the paste is poured into the pan for baking.

10–12 PORTIONS

4 shallots
2 garlic cloves
1 tbsp butter
2 tbsp cognac
⅓ cup (75 ml) red wine
1 lb (500 g) veal liver or calf liver
10½ oz (300 g) fresh bacon
5 anchovy fillets
3 tbsp wheat flour
1⅓ cups (300 ml) whipping cream
4 eggs
1 tbsp Swedish light syrup or Lyle's Golden Syrup
1 tbsp Japanese soy sauce
1 tsp white wine vinegar
½ tbsp salt
black pepper to taste
½ tbsp dried sage
1 tsp ground coriander
¼ tsp cayenne pepper
3 tbsp pickled capers (drain before use)
butter for the pan

1. Preheat the oven to 350°F (175°C). Peel and chop the onion and garlic finely. Fry in a frying pan with butter but do not allow them to brown. Pour in the cognac and red wine and cook until all the liquid evaporates.

2. Cut the liver and bacon into coarse pieces.

3. Mix the liver, bacon, onion, garlic, and anchovies until you get a smooth paste (you can also run everything twice through a meat grinder with the finest blade).

4. Whisk together the flour, cream, eggs, syrup, soy sauce, vinegar, salt, and spices and add a little at a time to the liver paste. Add capers.

5. Grease the bottom of a pan with generous amounts of butter. Pour the paste into the pan, but don't let it reach all the way to the top rim.

6. Place the pan on a long sheet filled with hot water and bake in the oven for 2 hours. Cover the pâté with aluminum foil as soon as it gains color. Remove from the oven and let cool.

7. Serve with Cumberland sauce and gherkins or pickles.

Confit of pork

This delicious dish takes time to make, but the result is tender and flavorful meat.

6–8 PORTIONS

approx. 2¼ lbs (1 kg) cured pork in pieces
some fresh sage leaves
4–5 garlic cloves
10–14 oz (300–400 g) duck or goose fat
2 tbsp butter
¼ cup (50 ml) dark beef stock
1 tsp salt, freshly ground black pepper

1. Preheat the oven to 200°F (90°C). Place the meat, sage, and garlic in a ovenproof baking pan and add the fat. Cover the pan with aluminum foil. Place in the oven and let stand for 12 hours.

2. Remove the meat and place it in a bowl under a weight in the fridge for about 12 hours.

3. Preheat the oven to 400°F (200°C). Place the meat in an ovenproof baking pan. Melt the butter and mix it with the stock, salt, and pepper. Pour the mixture over the meat and let it stand in the middle of the oven for about 1 hour. Serve the confit of pork warm or cold, as a topping for a meaty sandwich or just with a salad.

Coleslaw
with herb mayonnaise

A deliciously green and mild coleslaw with mixed herb mayonnaise. Mayonnaise doesn't need to be all that difficult to make. Especially not if it requires the whole egg, as is used here. Bring out all the ingredients in advance so they're all the same temperature.

4–6 PORTIONS

1 head of white cabbage (approx. 12 oz / 350 g)
HERB MAYONNAISE:
2 garlic cloves
1 egg
¾–1¼ cups (200–300 ml) fresh herbs, for example basil, mint, cilantro, parsley
½ tsp salt
2 tbsp apple cider vinegar
¾ cup (200 ml) neutral Canola oil
1 lemon, zest

1. Finely sliver the cabbage. Use a cheese grater or a mandolin.

2. Peel and mince the garlic.

3. Mix the egg, garlic, herbs, salt, and vinegar with an immersion blender or in a food processor.

4. Add oil in a thin stream while mixing. Mix in the lemon zest and add salt to taste.

5. Mix the cabbage with the herb mayonnaise. Let the coleslaw stand in the fridge for a few hours.

HYACINTH GARLAND

Decorate the Christmas table with fragrant garlands.

You need: Hyacinth, steel wire, wire cutters.

Remove the hyacinth blossoms from the stem. Thread the blossoms onto a piece of steel wire.

Root vegetable salad

This wintry salad looks fresh and beautiful in delicate pastels and is a good accompaniment to most dishes.

4–6 PORTIONS

1 chiogga beet or red beetroot
1 yellow beet
1 carrot
1 fennel
½ pomegranate
DRESSING:
4 tbsp olive oil
½ lemon, juice
½ tsp salt

1. Peel the chiogga beet, yellow beet, and carrot and grate them roughly. Cut the fennel into thin slices. Seed the pomegranate (see p. 118). Put everything in a bowl.

2. Mix the dressing and pour it over the salad. Mix well.

Apple and walnut salad

The perfect Christmas salad! Apples and walnuts are the best flavor buddies of the Christmas ham. Change up the salad by adding thinly sliced celery or fennel and/or chopped, dried cranberries.

4 PORTIONS

1 head of lettuce, leaf lettuce, frisée, arugula, or endive lettuce
2 red apples
1 avocado
1 handful of walnuts
DRESSING:
3 tbsp walnut or olive oil
1½ tsp mustard
1 tsp water
salt and pepper

1. Rinse the lettuce and break or cut into strips.

2. Cut the apples in half and core them. Cut them into thin slices. Cut the avocado in half and remove the pit. Dice the avocado. Chop the walnuts roughly. Combine the apple, avocado, and walnuts in a salad bowl.

3. Mix the ingredients for the dressing, add salt and pepper to taste, and drizzle it over the salad. Mix well.

The Fruit-bearing Pomegranate.

TO SEED A POMEGRANATE

It can be a little tricky to remove the seeds from a pomegranate. To make them come out easier, you can carefully press on the outside before cutting the pomegranate. Another good method to prevent the red juice from splashing all over the kitchen is to remove the seeds underwater. Cut the pomegranate and hold each piece underwater while picking out the seeds—which will sink to the bottom while the thin white "walls" float to the surface.

Orange salad
sultan's jewels

Fresh, beautiful, and vibrant! An orange salad lights up the Christmas table and goes well among all the hearty and somewhat fatty dishes. Serve with the meat or as an intermediate course.

4 PORTIONS

3–4 oranges
½ red onion
½ pomegranate
1 handful of pistachios
freshly ground black pepper
DRESSING:
¼ cup (50 ml) olive oil
2 tbsp freshly squeezed lemon juice
¼ tsp salt
freshly ground black pepper
½ tsp ground cumin

1. Peel and slice the oranges. Place them on a large serving dish as in the photo adjacent.

2. Peel and slice the onion thinly and place the rings on top of the oranges.

3. Divide the pomegranate and seed it (see adjacent inset).

4. Mix all the ingredients for the dressing.

5. Place the pomegranate seeds and pistachios atop the oranges and drizzle the dressing on last. Let it stand in the fridge for a little while.

Avocado and grapefruit salad

A fresh salad with the best imports of the season: citrus and avocado.

2–4 PORTIONS, AS AN ACCOMPANIMENT

1 pink grapefruit
1 avocado
1 head of romaine lettuce
olive oil, preferably a fruity Greek one
salt to taste
freshly ground black pepper

1. Cut off the peel of the grapefruit with a sharp knife. Cut out segments from the fruit (see p. 146) or cut it into thin slices. Save the juice.

2. Halve the avocado and remove the pit, then cut into rough pieces.

3. Tear the lettuce roughly and arrange the leaves on a large serving dish. Arrange the grapefruit and avocado on it and pour the grapefruit juice over top.

4. Drizzle the olive oil in circles over the salad and season with salt and pepper.

A variety of Christmas meatballs

Everyone has an opinion about what type of meatballs are the tastiest—therefore we've suggested several different styles. You can choose, or experiment to find your own favorite flavor. Let the ground meat stand in the fridge for an hour—this will make it easier to fry. Fry a quick sample and adjust the seasoning. The meatballs can be made 1–2 days in advance. Heat them in the microwave (on half power) or in the oven at 200°F (100°C) before serving. Some prefer cold meatballs, and that's not a bad option either.

APPROX. 50 MEATBALLS

2¼ lbs (1 kg) mixed ground meat (half ground beef, half ground pork)
½ cup (100 ml) breadcrumbs
¾ cup (200 ml) whipping cream
1 tbsp salt
2 eggs
butter and oil for the frying
SEASONING 1:
1 tbsp Swedish sweet mustard (available at IKEA or online)
½ tsp freshly ground nutmeg
½ tsp ground coriander seeds
SEASONING 2:
1 tbsp paprika powder
1 tsp ground allspice
SEASONING 3:
freshly ground white and black pepper
1 finely grated onion
SEASONING 4:
2¾ oz (80 g) finely chopped bacon, fried
2 tsp dried thyme

1. Mix the breadcrumbs and whipping cream and let stand for 10 minutes.

2. Mix the breadcrumb mixture with the ground meat, salt, one of the seasonings, and the eggs. Stir until the meat becomes a little gooey. Test fry a small amount and taste. Let the meat stand in the fridge for a little while.

3. With wet hands, shape the meat into about 50 meatballs. A tablespoon of ground meat is about right for one meatball. Place the meatballs on a tray or a baking sheet rinsed in cold water.

4. Fry the meatballs in batches in butter and oil over high heat until they attain a nice color. Shake the pan every now and then. The frying time is 4–5 minutes. Let cool. Serve with lingonberry jam.

Meatballs
with apple and cranberries

A nice way to spiff up the meatballs on the Christmas table.

8 SMALL PORTIONS

1 batch of meatballs with flavoring (see recipe to the left)
2–3 tbsp butter
3–4 apples
½–¾ cup (100–200 ml) cranberries or lingonberries

1. Fry the meatballs carefully in a frying pan with butter.

2. Seed the apples and cut them into wedges (the skin should remain on). Put them in the pan and let fry for a couple of minutes until they're shiny.

3. Add berries and let them warm up. Serve immediately (or set aside and heat up when you're ready to serve).

Extra delicious prinskorv sausage

Don't be stingy when you're buying prinskorv—Sweden's traditional Christmas sausage. Buy organic sausages with high meat content.

8 SMALL PORTIONS

16 prinskorv sausages (can be found at IKEA, online, or even homemade)
1 tbsp butter
1 finely chopped red onion
1 finely diced yellow or orange bell pepper
1 tbsp olive oil
1 diced tomato
a little salt
freshly ground black pepper
1 tbsp finely chopped parsley

1. Cut an X into the ends of the sausages.

2. Fry the sausages slowly in butter over low heat. They'll open up a little like bouquets at the ends. Set aside and keep warm.

3. Fry the onion and bell peppers in olive oil. When the vegetables soften, add the diced tomato. Add salt and pepper and sprinkle parsley on top. Pour the fried contents on top of the sausages and serve immediately.

Pork ribs
with sage, marjoram, and lemon

Deliciously juicy ribs are a classic warm dish on the Christmas table. Sage is a traditional winter herb, and is here complemented by marjoram and some refreshing lemon.

6−8 SMALL PORTIONS

4½ lbs (2 kg) thick pork ribs, preferably with rind
1 lemon
1 tbsp salt
freshly ground white pepper
1 tsp dried sage
1 tsp dried marjoram

1. Preheat the oven to 400°F (200°C). Squeeze the lemon over the ribs and rub the ribs with salt and herbs.

2. Roast the meat for 30 minutes or until it gets a nice color. Then reduce the temperature to 300°F (150°C) ° and cook for another hour or until the meat comes off the bone.

3. Cut the meat into small pieces. If you want, clean the pan with a little water and serve the gravy with the meat. Applesauce goes great with it.

Low temperature ribs

For those who prefer, you can roast the ribs at 100−125° for 3−4 hours. This way they become juicier but are not as crispy.

Ginger ribs

Swap the seasoning for 2 tbsp ground ginger or 2 tbsp finely chopped fresh ginger, which can be combined with sage or with nothing at all.

Pork ribs
varnished with glaze

The trick with these ribs is that they are first simmered in stock until tender and then glazed with a strong, sweet glaze.

8 SMALL PORTIONS

2¾ lbs (1¼ kg) thin pork ribs
1 batch of Yule glaze (see the next recipe)
8.5 cups (1 liter) veal stock

1. Begin by making the glaze (see below).

2. Boil the broth in a spacious pot, add the ribs, and let simmer carefully while covered for about 20 minutes. Let cool. Save the broth (it can become a dip or soup).

3. Preheat the oven to 450°F (225°C). Brush the ribs all over with the glaze and roast them until they get a nice color. Brush one more time after about 15 minutes. Roasting should take about 25 minutes. Serve the ribs warm or cooled.

Yule glaze

Here we have put together a bunch of Christmas ingredients—figs, raisins, dates, mustard, vinegar, and ginger—along with other fun things. It becomes a thick barbecue-inspired sauce, or glaze, which can be brushed on pre-simmered spareribs.

8 SMALL PORTIONS

¾ cup (200 ml) tomato ketchup + ½ cup (100 ml) chili sauce
1 tbsp Swedish sweet mustard (available at IKEA or online)
2 tbsp granulated sugar
2 tbsp white vinegar
2 tsp Worcestershire sauce
2 tbsp Japanese soy sauce
½ cup (100 ml) honey
¼ cup (50 ml) dried figs
¼ cup (50 ml) raisins
4 dates
freshly ground black pepper
1 tbsp finely chopped fresh ginger
1¼ cups (300 ml) water

1. Combine all the ingredients in a thick bottomed pot and bring to boil. Cover and let simmer for about 20 minutes. Dilute with water if the sauce gets too thick.

2. Mix the sauce with hand mixer for about 30 seconds. Carefully add salt to taste. The sauce keeps in the fridge for at least 2 weeks.

Oven omelet

Oven-baked omelets are common on many Swedish Christmas tables, particularly in restaurants. Here we have combined Swedish goat cheese with a soft shrimp stew—it is really delicious. The omelet is fluffiest and tastiest when freshly made, but it can also be heated in the oven for 10 minutes before serving. If you want it to be completely vegetarian, you can stew 3.5 oz (100 g) of fresh spinach instead of the shrimp. It's just as delicious, but in a different way.

4–6 SMALL PORTIONS

OMELET:
4 eggs
1 egg yolk
¼ tsp salt
½ cup (100 ml) whipping cream
1 tsp thyme
¼–½ tsp cayenne pepper
freshly ground black pepper
1¾ oz (50 g) Swedish goat cheese, preferably a bit creamy
1 tbsp olive oil
STEW:
½ cup (100 ml) whipping cream
½ cup (100 ml) peeled shrimp
1 tsp squeezed lemon
salt to taste

1. Preheat the oven to 400°F (200°C). Stir together the eggs, egg yolk, salt, cream, thyme, cayenne pepper, and black pepper.

2. Cut the cheese slices ¼ inch (½ cm) thick. Grease an ovenproof dish with olive oil. Place the cheese slices in the dish and pour the omelet batter all around.

3. Bake the omelet in the oven for 15–20 minutes until it has just solidified.

4. Simmer the cream in a thick bottomed pot until two thirds remain. Put the shrimp in and bring to a boil. Add lemon and salt to taste.

5. Pour the stew over the omelet and serve.

Christmas pike

In Roslagen and the Finnish archipelago—among other places—pike used to be served at Christmas, usually with horseradish sauce. In the archipelago of Åboland, they put turnips and potato in the broth, as well as allspice—the recipe here follows this tradition. In order to be sure of getting the pike in time for Christmas dinner, it was caught a few weeks prior to Christmas. It was then kept in a marsh until it was needed.

4–6 PORTIONS

1 pike (4½–5½ lbs / 2–2½ kg)
10–12 medium-sized potatoes
1 turnip
1 large yellow onion
2 tbsp cooking salt
10 allspice berries
HORSERADISH SAUCE:
2 tbsp butter
2 tbsp wheat flour
4¼ cups (1 liter) broth from the boiled pike
½ cup (100 ml) whipping cream
1–2 tbsp fresh, grated horseradish
freshly ground white pepper
salt

1. Peel the potatoes. Peel and slice the turnip, peel and cut the onion into wedges. Place in a spacious pot.

2. Clean and cut the pike into portion-sized pieces across the back but so that the belly is still held together. Place the pike on top of the vegetables. Salt.

3. Pour in just enough cold water to cover the fish. Bring to a boil and skim. Add the allspice. Cover with a lid and let simmer over very low heat for about 1 hour.

4. Fry the butter and flour for the sauce, pour in the broth from the boiled pike while stirring, and let cook until it thickens. Pour in the cream and let simmer for a couple of minutes.

5. Add the horseradish and the freshly ground white pepper to taste. Perhaps add a little salt if needed. Serve fish, vegetables, and sauce immediately.

Jens' Christmas

When my sister and I were young the family sometimes celebrated Christmas at Grandma and Grandpa's house in Halmstad. There was something special about that. They had candles and clear, colored paper chains in the Christmas tree, and you could smell soap on the stairs and cloves in the kitchen.

Grandmother would place her own lutfisk in big containers in the dark, cold laundry room. She would deep fry crullers, make spiced meat roll, and bake cookies. On Christmas, Swedish Julmust, Pilsner, poached pears, and plums would be brought out of the pantry, and the Christmas table was filled with trays and casseroles with kale, onion sausage, creamy liver sausage, cheddar and bleu cheese from Kvibille.

My parents brought these traditions with them to their home in Bollmora, a suburb of Stockholm, and presented a similar Christmas table there. Now I'm the one carrying on this tradition. I love pickled herring, the subtle green flavor of kale, salted ham, homemade liver pâté, crispy and sugar sprinkled crullers, and chewy caramels. I craft these with heaping tablespoons of sentimentality and winter romance. White Christmases and chorus numbers stream from the sound system and a black and white classics play on the TV.

But Christmas isn't a closed tradition. It has been in constant flux for more than a thousand years and is enriched today by food from all the corners of the earth. The old does not exclude the new, so in my Christmas arrangement sashimi shares the table with gravlax and the pork ribs get a wilder flavor with fresh ginger instead of powdered. Christmas should be something out of the ordinary. This is when it truly becomes a joyous celebration even though blizzards gust outside.

Halland långkål

In Halland and large parts of Skane, kale has long been a traditional Christmas dish. Today, this delicate dish is eaten by kale lovers all over the country. The kale used to be boiled in pork broth and browned in lard. Later on, cream came to be added, which makes the flavor a little more mild. You can choose from different broths and fats—the most important thing is that the kale has a soft but still supple texture and that it is quite salty.

4–6 PORTIONS

2 large heads of kale
pork broth, ham broth, or beef stock
butter, lard, or pork fat
⅔ cup (150 ml) whipping cream
1 pinch of granulated sugar or a little syrup, optional
salt
freshly ground white pepper

1. Rinse the kale and tear the leaves from the stalks. Boil the kale in broth or stock until soft, about 30 minutes.

2. Remove the kale and let the water drain (set aside the stock in the meantime).

3. Chop the kale and fry it in the fat for quite some time. Add salt and pepper, and possibly add sugar or a little syrup. Dilute with some of the boiled stock (you can save the rest for making soup) and let it boil.

4. Dilute with cream and let that soak in as well. Add salt and pepper to taste.

Brown kale

When you brown the kale carefully you get a sweet and delicious flavor.

8 SMALL PORTIONS

1 head of white cabbage
5 tbsp butter
4 tbsp Swedish light syrup or Lyle's Golden Syrup
2 cups (500 ml) pork broth or beef stock

1. Cut away the root of the cabbage and shred the cabbage.

2. Brown the cabbage in butter in a lard pot. Add salt and pepper, and pour in the syrup and pork broth. Simmer carefully for about 30 minutes.

3. Pour in more water if the kale is about to boil dry. Taste. Serve the brown kale warm.

Red cabbage

A healthy, classic cabbage dish for the Christmas table.

8 SMALL PORTIONS

½ head of red cabbage (17 oz / 500 g)
2 tbsp butter
1 tbsp red wine vinegar
1 large tart apple
1½ tsp salt
¼ tsp freshly ground black pepper
½ cup (100 ml) redcurrant juice or blackcurrant juice

1. Sliver the cabbage with a knife (or use a cheese grater or mandolin).

2. Fry the cabbage in the butter in a large pot. Add the vinegar.

3. Grate the peeled apple into the cabbage. Season with salt, pepper, and dilute with the redcurrant juice.

4. Let the cabbage simmer while covered for 20–30 minutes. Taste.

Red cabbage salad

The combination of sesame and cabbage is lovely.

8 SMALL PORTIONS

¼ head of red or white cabbage
approx. 2 inches of radish
1 tart apple, optional
½ tsp salt
1 tsp squeezed lemon
1 tsp sesame oil
1 tbsp olive oil

1. Sliver the cabbage finely. Peel and cut the radish into thin slices, which in turn should be divided into quarters. Put the cabbage and radish in a bowl and add salt, lemon juice, and sesame oil as well as olive oil.

2. Stir and let stand at room temperature for half an hour. Then, place in fridge until ready to serve.

Oven-baked Brussels sprouts
with lemon and garlic

It took Johanna many years to befriend the Brussels sprout, but they are now basically best buddies. Especially when the Brussels sprout has taken a bit of a dip in this marinade and been roasted in the oven until crispy. The lemon lightens up the presentation.

4–6 PORTIONS

1 lb (500 g) Brussels sprouts
2–3 garlic cloves
3 tbsp olive oil
1 lemon, zest and juice
salt and pepper

1. Preheat the oven to 350°F (180°C).

2. Clean the sprouts and cut them in half. Mince the garlic.

3. Stir together the oil, lemon juice, lemon zest, and the minced garlic. Turn the Brussels sprouts in the oil. Let them marinate for half an hour.

4. Place all the ingredients in an ovenproof dish. Add salt and pepper. Place in oven and bake for 18–20 minutes. Stir once.

5. Serve the Brussels sprouts hot or warm.

Sautéed Brussels sprouts
in Italian company

Boiled in veal stock, these Brussels sprouts get a rounder and full-bodied flavor. The dish becomes extra luxurious with thyme and roasted pine nuts, or try a little gremolata on top (see p. 160).

4–6 PORTIONS

17 oz (500 g) Brussels sprouts
3½ oz (100 g) pancetta or bacon
1 small shallot
1 garlic clove
2 tbsp olive oil
2 tbsp butter
¼ cup (50 ml) white wine
⅔ cup (150 ml) veal stock
FOR SERVING:
fresh thyme, roasted pine nuts, olive oil, and balsamic
**   vinegar (optional)**

1. Rinse and clean the sprouts. Cut the pancetta or bacon into fine strips. Peel and mince the onion and garlic.

2. Heat the oil and butter in a frying pan with high edges. Add the Brussels sprouts and shake them around in the pan. Reduce the heat and cook the Brussels sprouts for 3–4 minutes.

3. Add the pancetta or bacon and fry until crispy. Add the onion and garlic and stir well. Fry until the onion is soft. Pour in the wine and let simmer until the liquid is reduced by half.

4. Pour in the veal stock and let everything simmer for 10 minutes. The Brussels sprouts should be soft but still have a little bite.

5. Serve with thyme, roasted pine nuts, olive oil, and a few drops of a high quality balsamic vinegar, if you like.

Jansson's Temptation

This classic often shows up toward evening as a light supper served with herring and schnapps. It feels extra festive if you prepare your Jansson in portion-sized pans.

4–6 PORTIONS

2¼ lbs (1 kg) firm potatoes
1 yellow onion
2 tins of sprats (or Swedish anchovies) (each 4½ oz / 125 g)
1¼ cups (300 ml) whipping cream
approx. 3½ tbsp (50 g) butter
3 tbsp breadcrumbs or panko

1. Preheat the oven to 450°F (225°C).

2. Peel and cut the potatoes into strips about a ¼ inch (½ cm) thick. Peel and slice the onion finely.

3. Remove the anchovies from the liquid in the tin and mix the liquid with the cream.

4. Grease an ovenproof dish with a small dab of butter. Layer the potato, onion, and sprats in the pan. Make sure that the top is a layer of potatoes. Pour the cream mix over top and sprinkle with breadcrumbs. Place a small dab of butter on top.

5. Place in the oven and bake for about 40 minutes. Put the Jansson's Temptation in the fridge until serving.

Hansson's Temptation

We'd love you to make a vegetarian version without the sprats. This is often appreciated by the younger guests.

Karlsson's Temptation

This is the name of a Jansson's Temptation with sautéed ground beef instead of sprats.

Anchovy-Jansson

A slightly piquant variety of Jansson. Since large portions aren't eaten it's very flavorful and has quite a high level of salt. You can sprinkle breadcrumbs on (at the same time as the butter), but we suggest that you skip that.

8 SMALL PORTIONS

2 yellow onions
1 tbsp of butter for the frying
35 oz (1 kg) potatoes
12 anchovy filets + liquid
¾ cup (200 ml) whipping cream
¾ cup (200 ml) milk
freshly ground black pepper
1 tsp salt
2 tbsp butter

1. Peel and slice the onion. Fry it in butter until soft, but don't brown.

2. Preheat the oven to 450°F (225°C). Peel the potatoes and cut them into strips.

3. Grease an ovenproof dish, about 4 x 6 inches, or 8 small ramekins, with butter.

4. Mix potatoes, onion, and anchovies (save the liquid) in a bowl. Pour the mixture in the pans.

5. Combine the cream, milk, anchovy liquid, black pepper, and salt. Pour half of the liquid into the pans.

6. Place all of it in the oven and bake for 20 minutes. Pour in the rest of the cream mixture. Add a small dab of butter. Bake for another 25 minutes until the gratin attains a nice color and the potatoes are soft.

7. Let cool. Place in the fridge and heat up carefully just before serving.

The opera singer Pelle Janzon (1844–1889) is one of many who have been credited with the honor of having invented the classic Jansson's Temptation. Another story goes that the dish got the name from a 1928 film.

Kale pie
with walnuts

A hearty pie made from the best of winter greens. A brilliant vegetarian option for the Christmas table and a great pie to serve to a large number of guests; just double the recipe and bake in a large pan.

6–8 PORTIONS

⅔ cup (150 g) butter
1½ cups (350 ml) sifted spelt flour approx. 2 tbsp ice cold water
FILLING:
9 oz (250 g) fresh kale
2 red onions
1 tbsp butter
approx. ½ tsp salt
ground grated black pepper to taste
7 oz (200 g) goat cheese
¾ cup (200 ml) walnuts, roughly chopped
CUSTARD:
3 eggs
¾ cup (200 ml) whipping cream
½ cup (100 ml) milk

1. Mix the butter and flour together quickly, preferably in a food processor. Add the water and continue to mix until you have a smooth dough. This should only take a few seconds. Let the dough rest in the fridge for 30 minutes.

2. Prepare the filling. Score and roughly chop the kale. Boil it in lightly salted water for 5–10 minutes. Let it drain in a colander.

3. Peel and slice the onion thinly. Fry the onion and the cabbage in a pat of butter over not too high heat. Add salt and pepper.

4. Preheat the oven to 400°F (200°C). Roll out the dough and place it in the pie pan. Prick the dough with a fork. Pre-bake the pie crust for 10 minutes.

5. Whisk together the ingredients for the custard.

6. Place the cabbage mix in the pre-baked pie crust. Sprinkle the goat cheese on top and pour the custard into the pan. Sprinkle the walnuts on top.

7. Bake the pie in the lower part of the oven for 35–40 minutes.

Spinach pie

This pie is also perfect with frozen spinach. In this case, you can skip the step about boiling and just fry the spinach and onion for a few minutes.

Jerusalem artichoke au gratin
the little mother's way

One of Johanna's mother's signature dishes. The green Christmases of recent years have allowed her to dig up Jerusalem artichokes from the vegetable garden the day before Christmas Eve to make this deliciously creamy gratin.

4 PORTIONS

1 lb (500 g) Jerusalem artichokes
½ lemon, juice + 2 cups (500 ml) water
butter
1 garlic clove
1⅔ cups (400 ml) whipping cream
½ tsp salt
½ cup (100 ml) grated Parmesan cheese
2–3 tbsp breadcrumbs or panko

1. Preheat the oven to 400°F (200°C).

2. Peel the Jerusalem artichokes and place them in a bowl with lemon water so they don't darken.

3. Grease an oven dish with a little butter. Cut the artichokes into quarter-inch-thick slices. Place in the pan.

4. Press the garlic clove into the cream and add salt and most of the Parmesan cheese. Pour the cream over the Jerusalem artichokes. Sprinkle breadcrumbs or panko on top and add the rest of the Parmesan cheese.

5. Place the pan in the middle of the oven and bake for 25–30 minutes. Use a fork to see if the Jerusalem artichokes are soft. Serve hot or warm.

Black salsify gratin
with goat cheese and pine nut crumble

Black salsify is sometimes unfairly called the poor man's asparagus. But in reality it's an elegant root vegetable with a subtle and delicate flavor. When you peel off the skin, it gives off a slightly gooey liquid, so peel under running cold water. If you cannot find black salsify, it can be substituted with parsnips.

4 PORTIONS

approx. 1 lb (500 g) black salsify or turnips
½ lemon, juice + 2 cups (500 ml) water
1 cup (250 ml) whipping cream
5⅓ oz (150 g) goat cheese
approx. 1 tbsp scored thyme leaves
¼ tsp salt
day old bread
olive oil
¼ cup (50 ml) pine nuts

1. Peel the black salsify under cold, running water. Place them in a bowl with lemon water so they don't darken.

2. Cut the salsify into sticks or dice them, and boil while covered in lightly salted water for 10 minutes.

3. Heat the cream in a pot. Crumble in the goat cheese and fresh thyme and stir until the cheese melts. Add a little salt.

4. Preheat the oven to 450°F (225°C).

5. Place the black salsify in a greased oven dish. Pour the sauce on top.

6. Crumble the bread until you have about ½ cup (100 ml) breadcrumbs. Add a little olive oil into the crumbs.

7. Chop half of the pine nuts and leave the rest whole. Mix the breadcrumbs and pine nuts and sprinkle it over the gratin. Place the dish in the oven and let it cook for about 15 minutes or until it's attained a nice color. Serve hot or warm.

Celeriac with Parmesan

A Waldorf salad that has gotten lost in the Italian quarter... The celeriac has a mild and refined flavor that gets a boost from the lemon and Parmesan.

4–6 PORTIONS

1 small celeriac
4 garlic cloves
olive oil
½ lemon, zest and juice
1 sprig of fresh rosemary
10–12 cherry tomatoes, cut in half
sea salt and black pepper
approx. 1½ oz (40 g) Parmesan
2–3 tbsp finely slivered basil

1. Peel the celeriac and rinse it thoroughly. Cut it into thin sticks or slices. Peel and mince the garlic cloves.

2. Brown and fry the celeriac in olive oil until soft. Put aside.

3. Pour another splash of olive oil into the frying pan. Carefully brown the minced garlic together with the lemon zest and rosemary until the garlic gets a bit of color. Add the celeriac and cherry tomatoes and pour in the lemon juice. Season with salt and pepper. Mix well and let all of it heat up.

4. Remove from the heat and grate some Parmesan on top. Sprinkle with some finely slivered basil.

Menu 1

Christmas for one or two

If you're on your own or it's just the two of you for Christmas, you may attempt to make a few really delicious dishes. Make a three course meal rather than a Christmas table and take the opportunity to make it luxurious with the season's shellfish!

_____

Smoked fish with whitefish roe sauce (see p. 105) or lobster salad (see p. 171)

Oven fried duckbreast with blackcurrants or lingonberries (see p. 167)

Jerusalem artichoke au gratin, the little mother's way (see p. 133)

Avocado and grapefruit salad (see p. 119)

½ batch Clementine sorbet with butterscotch cookies (see p. 146)

Menu 2

Vegetarian Christmas

Of course, Christmas is traditionally full of meat, and because of that a classic Christmas table can easily look a little monochrome. That's unfortunate, because the season offers a lot of tasty things that are green—such as green cabbage and Brussels sprouts and all manner of lovely citrus fruits!

_____

Vegetarian Jansson, the so-called Hansson's Temptation (see p. 130), or Black salsify gratin with goat cheese and pine nut crumble (see p. 134)

Red cabbage salad (see p. 127)

Sautéed Brussels sprouts in Italian company (see p. 128)

Orange salad—the Sultan's jewels (see p. 119)

White cabbage salad with herb mayonnaise (see p. 117)

Poached pears as you want, with whipped cream (see p. 142)

If you want a "vegetarian" Christmas ham you can peel and boil a whole celeriac in broth and then glaze it in a classic manner (see recipe on how to glaze on p. 111)

Delicious breads and cheeses work nicely on the vegetarian Christmas table and please do use a few fresh picked greens such as radishes, pickled onions, and carrot sticks.

Menu 3

Christmas on a budget

Inviting the entire family to an enormous Christmas dinner or shopping for everything last minute can easily become an expensive affair. If you want to hold onto your money make sure to get in and out the grocery store in good time. Make your own preserves, meatballs, and gratins in advance and freeze them. And instead of a banquet, go for a few delicious dishes.

_____

Herring and Baltic herring in every way (see p. 98–102)

Gravlax or preserved salmon (see p. 106 or 160)

Root vegetable salad (see p. 117)

Kale, brown kale, or red cabbage (see p. 127)

Meatballs (see p. 121)

Oven omelet with goat cheese and shrimp (see p. 124)

Ris à la Malta (see p. 140)

FAST FOOD

Quickly prepared Christmas

If you've stayed out till the last minute but still want to arrange a swanky Christmas table you'll have to go for quick, simple, and delicious dishes and a couple ready-made items to spiff up.

_____

Preserved herring (see p. 98)

Egg halves to your liking (see p. 109)

Cured salmon with fennel and lemon (see p. 105)

Leg of mutton or other smoked meat

Readymade meatballs to be jazzed up

Apple and walnut salad (see p. 117)

Brussels sprouts—oven-baked and garlic fragranced

(use frozen that have been cleaned and are ready to go, see p. 128)

Celeriac with Parmesan (see p. 134)

Tiramisu semifreddo (see p. 153)

AVAILABLE IN A
can

Quick tips for Christmas

✳ Use store-bought pre-marinated herring (preferably from Sweden) and add some fresh ingredients. Add thinly sliced red onion or finely chopped dill or chives to the preserve. Save a little to sprinkle on top.

✳ Rub some readymade gravlax with a little cognac, whisky, or mulled wine and it will get an extra boost of flavor.

✳ Buy the ham readymade, but glaze it yourself.

✳ Choose some high quality meats at the store; it doesn't take any more time than when buying lesser quality. Watch out for milk powder and too many E numbers in the products you buy, and make sure that smoked products really are smoked properly. Don't forget that pâtés and the like should be served with some accompaniments such as pickled cucumber, Cumberland sauce, or whatever else you prefer.

✳ Fry the prinskorv sausages slowly in the pan. They become so much tastier that way and can be left to cook while you do other things.

✳ Skip the potatoes. Who wants to eat filling food on Christmas? Buy really delicious black rye bread and wort bread instead.

✳ Create an unmixed salad (with all the ingredients in small groups or rows on a large plate) by assembling everything you have in the fridge that will fit in a salad. There's usually more in the vegetable bin than what you suppose.

✳ Place the mustard, oil, vinegar, salt, and pepper on the table so everyone can serve themselves.

✳ Buy readymade Mandelmusslor cookies. Whip some cream and mix with berries. The result is tasty, pretty, and quick.

✳ Decorate the Christmas table with fruit—citrus fruits, pomegranates, and small red apples—and voila! Immediate Christmas ambience.

✳ Accept help by letting your guests and family bring food and drink.

After the salty and sometimes quite heavy food of Christmas, it can be nice to end with something sweet—at Christmastime, you can never have enough sweets! But also take the opportunity to revel in the season's sweet oranges and tangerines. Make the classic ris à la Malta with a modern twist. Round the meal off with ice cream, granita, or semifreddo. Bake a delightfully heavy chocolate cake, or finish with cheese. There's a grand finale here for everyone.

The fifth course
and other Christmas desserts

Ris à la Malta

in many ways

Originally, this dish was flavored only with almonds. Then it became popular to flavor it with orange. The creamy base is perfect for flavoring with all sorts of fruits and berries. It's common to use leftover rice pudding for ris à la Malta. The rice recipe is equivalent to 4 ½ cups (1 liter) of cold rice pudding.

6–8 SMALL PORTIONS

THE PUDDING:
2 quarts (2 liters) water
1¼ cups (300 ml) pudding rice
1⅔ cups (400 ml) whipping cream
3 tbsp powdered sugar or granulated sugar
FLAVORINGS:
- **3 oranges, peeled and cut into pieces**
- **3 blood oranges, peeled and cut into pieces**
- **4 tangerines, peeled and cut into pieces**
- **3½ oz (100 g) frozen blackberries, thawed**
- **3½ (100 g) frozen raspberries, thawed + some chopped mint leaves**
- **3½ (100 g) frozen blueberries**
- **3½ (100 g) frozen cloudberries and ¼ cup (50 ml) roughly chopped hazelnuts**
- **¾ cup (200 ml) pineapple chunks**
- **¾ cup (200 ml) sweet jam of choice**
- **1 tbsp vanilla sugar**
- **½ cup (100 ml) almond flakes**

1. Boil the water in a thick bottomed pot. Add the rice and boil until soft. This will take about 20 minutes.

2. Drain the water and rinse the rice carefully so it is cool. Let it drain properly in a sieve.

3. Whip the cream with the sugar. Add the rice to the cream and add flavoring of your choice. Sample and add a little more powdered sugar if required. Serve ris à la Malta as is or with matching berry sauce.

Ris à la crème brûlée

Sprinkle a little raw sugar over the ris à la Malta and let the sugar melt in the oven at 475°F (250°C) or use a kitchen blowtorch.

Ris à l'amande

Denmark's answer to ris à l'amande. Preferably serve with the cherry compote on page 145.

4–6 PORTIONS

2–2½ cups (500–600 ml) whipping cream
7 oz (200 g) blanched and peeled almonds (see p. 57)
1¾–2 cups (400–500 ml) cooked rice pudding
¼ cup (50 ml) granulated sugar
3 finely grated bitter almonds

1. Whip the cream lightly and roughly chop the almonds.

2. Mix half of the cream with the rice pudding, sugar, and both sweet and bitter almonds. Mix well so it becomes completely even and smooth. Then, carefully fold in the rest of the cream. Cover properly and place in the fridge until the ris à l'amande is to be eaten.

3. Serve with cherry compote or readymade cherry jam.

Poached pears your way

Poached pears are very tasty and juicy. Here we've collected different versions of this dessert. The amount of sugar is always approximated, since different types of pears have varying degrees of sweetness.

4–6 PORTIONS

5–6 firm small pears
LEMON PEAR:
1¼ cups (300 ml) raw or granulated sugar
1¼ cups (300 ml) water
1 lemon, zest and juice
LINGONBERRY OR CRANBERRY PEAR:
¾ cup (200 ml) granulated sugar
1¼ cups (300 ml) water
1⅔ cups (400 ml) lingonberries or cranberries, fresh or frozen, thawed
1 lemon, juice, optional
RASPBERRY PEAR:
¾ cup (200 ml) granulated sugar
1¼ cups (300 ml) water
¾ cup (200 ml) raspberries
raspberries for garnish, optional
BLUEBERRY PEAR:
½ cup (100 ml) granulated sugar
1¼ cups (300 ml) water
1¼ cups (300 ml) blueberries
1 lemon, juice, optional
blueberries for garnish, optional
RED WINE PEAR:
¾ cup (175 ml) granulated sugar
¾ cup (200 ml) red wine
6 black peppercorns
1 piece bitter orange peel
GINGER AND VANILLA PEAR:
2 cups (500 ml) water
¾ cup (200 ml) granulated sugar
a little more than 1 inch of fresh ginger, grated
1 lemon, zest
½ slit vanilla bean, or ½ tsp vanilla extract
1 cinnamon stick

1. Peel the pears, but keep the stem. Ideally, cut off a little of the base of the pear so it will stand up.

2. Begin by preparing the things to boil. Mix the sugar, water, and the flavoring you've chosen in a tall, heavy bottomed pot. Let simmer for about 5 minutes.

3. Add the pears. Simmer while covered for 10–30 minutes, depending on how soft and large the pears are.

4. Remove the pears when they're soft and place them in a bowl to cool. Or place them in glass jars if you plan to save them and to eat later.

5. Serve the pears with a lightly whipped cream and chopped, roasted nuts (see p. 151), or with butterscotch cookies (see p. 146).

Poached clementines

When citrus fruits are at their best, revel in them! The tangerines are given a licorice-like flavor from the star anise.

4–6 PORTIONS

4–6 clementines
SYRUP:
1¼ cups (300 ml) water
¾ cup (200 ml) granulated sugar
2 cinnamon sticks
2 star anise
½ vanilla bean or ½ tsp vanilla extract

1. Boil all the ingredients for the syrup. Let simmer for about 5 minutes.

2. Peel the clementines with a knife. Place them either whole or sliced in the syrup and let simmer for about 5 minutes. Set the pot aside and let cool.

3. Serve the clementines with a little whipped cream, ice cream, or in a glass of sparkling wine.

Poached kumquats

Small, sweetly acidic fruits that pair nicely with ice cream or can be used to decorate a chocolate cake. They keep in the fridge for 1–2 weeks.

2–3 JARS

approx. 1 lb (500 g) kumquats
the syrup from the recipe above

1. Rinse the kumquats carefully. Cut them into halves and remove the seeds. Place the kumquats in a pot and cover with water. Bring to boil and let simmer for 30 minutes.

2. Drain thoroughly in a colander.

3. Boil the syrup from the recipe above. Add the kumquats and let them simmer in the syrup for 15 minutes. Set the pot aside and let cool.

4. Pour into clean glass jars.

PERFECTLY CLEAN JARS

Wash the glass jars that you're going to use and let them dry. Place them on a rack in a cold oven, and set the oven to 200°F (100°C). Let the jars stand in the oven for 15 minutes or until you're ready to fill them.

Smålandish cheesecake

Don't be scared by the amount of milk and the hassle of finding rennet to make this dish. It's worth all that extra effort! A little much after a heavy Christmas dinner perhaps, but it makes a perfect snack after a day on the ski slopes or as a late supper on Christmas Eve. Adding raspberry or strawberry jam is tasty, but with cherry compote it's absolutely irresistible.

8 PORTIONS

½ cup (100 ml) wheat flour
3 quarts (3 liters) whole milk
1½ tbsp rennet (can be bought at most pharmacies)
4 eggs
½ cup (100 ml) granulated sugar
1¼ cups (300 ml) whipping cream
a pinch of salt
2 bitter almonds
20 blanched and peeled almonds (see p. 57)

1. Mix the flour with about ½ cup (100 ml) of the milk and whisk it smooth.

2. Heat the rest of the milk until it is 99°F (37°C). Mix the flour paste and rennet and stir well. Let the milk stand for about 1 hour.

3. Preheat the oven to 350°F (175°C).

4. Stir the milk so that it separates properly. Pour the separated milk into a cooking strainer with a cheese cloth and strain the buttermilk from the cheese. You can also pick out the cheese with a skimmer. (The buttermilk can be saved and used for baking bread if you want.)

5. Mix the eggs, sugar, cream, and salt in a bowl. Grate the bitter almonds into it.

6. Chop the almonds and mix them and the cheese into the cream mix. Stir well.

7. Pour it all into a greased ovenproof dish and place in the oven. Bake for 50–60 minutes until the surface is golden and the center has solidified.

8. Serve the cheesecake warm with whipped cream and jam or with the cherry compote on the side.

Cherry compote

If you're not lucky enough to have a cherry tree in your garden or a freezer full of cherries, then you can always find the cherries for a delicious compote in the freezer aisle. And if you can't find any frozen cherries, simply serve a delicious cherry jam with the cheese cake. The refreshing tartness of the berries contrasts nicely against the creamy cheesecake.

8 PORTIONS

7 oz (200 g) frozen cherries
½ cup (100 ml) granulated sugar
1 vanilla bean or 1 tsp vanilla extract
1 tbsp potato flour, optional

1. Combine the cherries and sugar in a pot. Make a slit along the vanilla bean and add it to the pot. Let the cherries boil up carefully and then simmer for 5–10 minutes over low heat. Remove the vanilla bean.

2. If you want a firmer compote, you can mix 1 tbsp potato flour in a little cold water and stir it into the warm cherry sauce.

Italian cheesecake

Make an Italian version of this cheesecake by swapping the milk and the whole section about making the cheese with 29 oz (250 g) of ricotta cheese. Mix the ricotta with the eggs, sugar, cream, salt, and flour in a bowl and then follow the recipe above. You can even add the zest from 1 lemon, as you're already Italianizing the dish.

Citrus salad

with star anise syrup

A really elegant fruit salad. Beautiful, tangy, tasty.

4–6 PORTIONS

**5–6 different citrus fruits, for example grapefruit,
orange, clementine, and lime**
STAR ANISE SYRUP:
½ cup (100 ml) granulated sugar
½ cup (100 ml) water
2–3 star anise

1. Cut off the peels from the citrus fruit—be careful to
remove the entire peel and the pith, which has a bitter
taste. Fillet the wedges (see below) with a sharp knife. Toss
the citrus pieces in a bowl.

2. Boil all the ingredients for the syrup in a pot and let
simmer for a few minutes. Remove from the heat and let
cool before pouring over the citrus fruits.

Clementine sorbet

with butterscotch cookies

*A fresh, cool, and simple end to a hearty Christmas dinner.
Remember that the sorbet should be served immediately
after it has been mixed together.*

4–6 PORTIONS

¼ cup (50 ml) granulated sugar
½ cup (100 ml) water
2 cinnamon sticks (can be omitted)
the juice of 5–6 clementines (approx. 3/4 cup / 200 ml juice)
2 egg whites
butterscotch cookies (see the recipe to the right)
clementine wedges

1. Boil the sugar, water, and if you like, the cinnamon sticks
in a pot. Set aside and let the sugar syrup cool.

2. Squeeze the juice from the tangerines—be sure to get as
much of the pulp as possible.

3. Mix the cooled sugar syrup with the tangerine juice and
distribute everything in an ice cube tray. Let it stand in the
freezer for at least 6 hours—preferably overnight.

4. Complete the sorbet just before ready to serve. Whisk
the egg whites into a stiff foam. Add the tangerine ice
cubes and mix the sorbet with a hand mixer or in a food
processor and run until it becomes a smooth sorbet.

5. Serve immediately in glasses with butterscotch cookies
and filleted clementine wedges (see description to the right).

Old style butterscotch cookies

*Crispy, crunchy cookies that make a good accompaniment
to cool, fresh desserts such as the clementine sorbet to the
left or for creamy ice cream and panna cotta. You can also
simply munch on them as is with a cup of coffee or with a
glass of sweet wine.*

APPROX. 15 BUTTERSCOTCH COOKIES

½ cup (100 ml) almond flakes
3½ tbsp (50 g) butter
¼ cup (50 ml) granulated sugar
1½ oz (40 g) glucose (2½ tbsp)

1. Preheat the oven to 300°F (150°C).

2. Place the almonds on a tray and roast them lightly—
they're only supposed to get some color.

3. Mix the butter, sugar, and glucose in a thick bottomed pot
and let it boil until it "glues together" and thickens. Stir
every now and then. Carefully mix in the roasted almonds.

4. Raise the oven temperature to 350°F (175°C).

5. Dollop the batter with even spacing on a tray lined with
parchment paper. Bake the cookies for about 5 minutes—
they're supposed to become vaguely light brown. Let them
cool a little, and then you can use a rolling pin or a glass
bottle to help form their shape.

6. Store the cookies in airtight containers, preferably on
paper towels. They are very brittle.

FILLETING CITRUS FRUIT

Cut away the outer peel and
the pith with a sharp knife.
Then carefully cut the meat of
the fruit out by inserting the
knife along the thin walls of
the membranes.

Grapefruit granita

Tart, cool, and refreshing. A perfect dessert or a palate cleanser for Christmastime.

APPROX. 8 PORTIONS

1¼ cups (300 ml) water
¾ cup (200 ml) granulated sugar
the juice from 3–4 grapefruits (approx. 2 cups / 500 ml)

1. Boil the water and sugar in a small pot until the sugar has dissolved. Let the syrup cool.

2. Squeeze the grapefruits and strain the juice. Pour the juice into the cooled sugar syrup. Pour it all into a small loaf pan. Let it stand in the freezer for at least 4 hours.

3. When you're about to serve the granita, scrape it out with a fork and place in portion bowls. Serve immediately.

Christmas cake of pan d'oro

In Italy, pan d'oro, or the fruit-filled variety panettone is always served at Christmas. It's a beautiful cake, but is rather bland on its own, so take the opportunity to fill it with something tasty. Cut it like a Christmas tree and you'll get a magnificent feast for the eyes on the Christmas table!

APPROX. 10 PIECES

1 Italian Christmas cake (pan d'oro)
2 packages of frozen raspberries (15 oz / 450 g)
1 cup (225 ml) granulated sugar
9 oz (250 g) mascarpone
¼ cup (50 ml) maraschino liqueur or orange liqueur,
**   such as Cointreau powdered sugar for garnish**

1. Cut the cake into slices—see picture to the right!

2. Stir the raspberry and sugar together. Mix the mascarpone with the liqueur (or with a little vanilla if you want an alcohol-free variety).

3. Spread a layer of mascarpone on the first slice and then a layer of raspberries. Top with another piece of cake. Continue in this way with the rest of the cake. Place the slices so they wrap around like a Christmas tree.

4. Let the cake stand in a cool place for about an hour so it has a chance to settle. Sprinkle powdered sugar on top just before serving.

ICE LANTERN

A beautiful winter lantern to place on the porch steps or the balcony. Decorate with beautiful holly leaves and sprigs. If you use distilled water, the lantern will be clearer.

You need: 1 large bucket or bowl + 1 small bucket or bowl, water, a weight (a rock or similar), sprigs, leaves and berries, candles.

1. Fill the large bowl halfway with water.

2. Place the smaller bowl inside and keep it in place with some form of weight. Stick the sprigs, leaves, and berries between the bowls.

3. Place the bowls outside for a few hours or overnight so they freeze. Or, if it's not cold enough outside, put them in the freezer.

4. Free the ice bowl from the molds. Pour a little warm water on the outside of the larger bowl and inside the smaller one to make it easier to remove.

5. Put a tea light candle in the ice lantern and light it.

Chocolate mousse

Smooth, creamy mousse made with fine chocolate is like enjoying a whole table full of treats in one spoonful.

4 PORTIONS

3½ oz (100 g) dark chocolate (70%)
¾ cup (200 ml) whipping cream
2 tbsp strong espresso coffee
2 egg yolks
candied citrus peel (see recipe below)

1. Melt the chocolate in a water bath (see p. 57)

2. Whip the cream until fluffy but not too stiff.

3. Stir in the coffee and stir one egg yolk at a time into the melted chocolate. Fold the chocolate into the whipped cream.

4. Dollop or use a pastry bag to pipe the mousse into glasses or bowls. Decorate with candied citrus peel (see recipe below) or butterscotch cookies on p. 146.

Candied citrus peel

Candied citrus peel is flavorful and beautiful on all Christmas desserts. You can even give it as a unique and lovely homemade Christmas gift.

APPROX. 1¼ CUPS (300 ML)

4 organic oranges or lemons
1 cup (250 ml) water
2 cups (500 ml) granulated sugar

1. Peel the oranges. Make sure to get rid of as much of the pith as possible—it tastes bitter.

2. Cut the peel into thin strips. Place the strips in a bowl and cover completely with boiling water. Let stand for 30 minutes and then drain the water.

3. Boil more water (1 cup / 250 ml) with the sugar. When the sugar has dissolved, add the orange peel and reduce the heat. Simmer for 15 minutes.

4. Remove the pot from the heat and cover with a lid. Let cool completely and then store the peel in the syrup. It can keep in the fridge for 2 weeks.

Chocolate cake

This wonderfully impressive chocolate cake reminds us of Italian Baci pralines and can even replace the entire candy table if you love dark chocolate. An extra plus is that the cake is gluten-free.

10–12 PIECES

7 oz (200 g) roasted hazelnuts (see below)
3½ oz (100 g) dark chocolate (70%)
6 eggs
½ cup (125 g) room temperature butter
1 jar of Nutella (14 oz / 400 g)
¼ tsp salt
1 tbsp butter + 1 tbsp cocoa powder for the pan
FROSTING:
3½ oz (100 g) dark chocolate (70%)
½ cup (100 ml) whipping cream

1. Preheat the oven to 350°F (180°C).

2. Grind half of the hazelnuts in a blender or with an almond grinder. Melt the chocolate in a water bath (see p. 57) or in a microwave.

3. Divide the eggs and place the eggs and yolks in separate bowls. Stir the butter into the bowl with the yolks and add the Nutella, ground hazelnuts, and salt.

4. Whisk the egg whites into a stiff foam and fold them into the chocolate batter. Mix carefully into an even batter.

5. Grease a springform pan with removable sides and shake 1 tbsp cocoa around in the pan. Pour in the batter and bake the cake for about 40 minutes. Let cool.

6. Chop the chocolate for the frosting. Heat up the cream and stir in the chocolate. Spread the frosting over the cake. Garnish with roasted hazelnuts.

ROASTED HAZELNUTS

If you can't find roasted hazelnuts in the store you can roast them yourself! Place the nuts on a tray. Place the tray in a cold oven and set the oven to 350°F (175°C). When the oven reaches the right temperature, the hazelnuts are usually done. Let them cool and then crack away the shell between your palms or with the help of a kitchen towel.

Candied apples

It was probably an American, William W. Kolb, who began making candied apples at the beginning of the 1900s. After that, these giant lollipops / candied apples on a stick have become a Halloween staple, both in the US and Great Britain. We have made our own Christmas version by boiling lingonberries and raspberries together with the sugar syrup.

12 PORTIONS

12 small red apples, not too sweet
12 wooden skewers or similar
oil for the pan
SYRUP:
2 cups (500 ml) granulated sugar
7 oz (200 g) frozen lingonberries or cranberries
3½ oz (100 g) frozen raspberries
¾ cup (200 ml) water

1. Grease a baking sheet with a little oil. Rinse the apples and dry them thoroughly, remove the stems, and stick a skewer in each apple.

2. Boil sugar, lingonberries, raspberries, and water in a thick bottomed pot—check the temperature on the syrup every now and then with a digital kitchen thermometer. Scrape the side of the pot with a spatula or a whisk so that no crystallized sugar sticks to the sides to make the syrup grainy.

3. Let the syrup boil until the temperature reaches 250°F (120°C) (that is to say, when it's reached the caramel stage), then remove the pot from the heat. Caution! Watch out, the syrup is really hot and can cause burns!

4. Dip one apple at a time into the syrup and then place them on the baking sheet to cool. You can also place the apples directly on the plate or tray they will be served on. Eat the apples like jumbo lollipops once they have cooled.

Tiramisu semifreddo

Two delicious Italian desserts in one go!

6–8 PORTIONS

3 eggs
½ cup (100 ml) granulated sugar
1 tbsp vanilla sugar (or vanilla extract)
9 oz (250 g) mascarpone
¾ cup (200 ml) whipping cream
10–15 lightly crushed almond macaroons
    or Italian Amaretti cookies
3½ oz (100 g) chopped dark chocolate (70%)
CHOCOLATE AND ESPRESSO SAUCE:
¼ cup (50 ml) espresso
¼ cup (50 ml) water
2 tbsp cocoa powder
1¾ oz (50 g) finely chopped dark chocolate (70%)
½ cup (100 ml) granulated sugar
½ cup (100 ml) whipping cream

1. Crack the eggs and separate the yolks from the whites. Place the yolks in one bowl and the whites in another. Pour sugar and vanilla sugar into the bowl with the yolks and whisk until fluffy. Stir in the mascarpone cheese.

2. Whisk the egg whites into a stiff foam in a clean bowl and whip the cream in another bowl. Carefully fold the cream and egg whites into the mascarpone mixture. Finally, mix in the crushed cookies and the chopped chocolate. Place the mixture in the freezer. Cover with plastic wrap; it should lie tight across the semifreddo. Let stand in the freezer for at least 3 hours.

3. Remove the semifreddo from the freezer about half an hour before it is to be served and place it in the fridge. It should be "semifreddo," which means semi-frozen in Italian.

4. Heat the espresso and water in a small pot. Stir in cocoa, dark chocolate, and sugar and stir until the chocolate melts.

5. Whisk in the cream and then let the sauce simmer while stirring until it thickens. Pour the warm sauce over the semifreddo. Serve immediately, preferably with some whole macaroons on top.

Äggost Jens' way

A classic from Bohuslän that lends a lovely rustic feeling to the Christmas table.

6 PORTIONS

2½ quarts (2½ liters) whole milk
1¼ cups (300 ml) whipping cream
1¼ cups (300 ml) sour cream
6 eggs
1 tsp white vinegar (12%)
2 tbsp granulated sugar or vanilla sugar

1. Heat the milk and cream just to the boiling point and remove immediately from the heat, so it doesn't boil over.

2. Whisk the sour cream and eggs and whisk this mixture into the cream. Heat while stirring until it separates. Add the vinegar.

3. Remove the pot from the heat and let it stand for about 30 minutes. Using a skimmer, lift up the granular mass and let it drain in an Äggost mold or in a round mesh strainer. Add a little sugar for each spoonful that is removed.

4. Let stand and drain over a bowl in the fridge overnight.

5. Tip the Äggost onto a tray and garnish with mashed lingonberries, cranberry sauce, or any lightly sweetened berries of choice.

Krukost

It's easy to mix together a krukost, also known as potkes—a type of traditional cheese spread. Serve it with bread and biscuits on the Christmas table. Caraway and other spices give the cheese an interesting character, but can be omitted if you want a purer flavor.

8–10 SMALL PORTIONS

5 oz (140 g) bleu cheese
14 oz (400 g) aged cheddar or sveciaost
⅔ cup (150 g) soft butter
2–4 tbsp cognac, Armagnac, or other flavorful liquor
1½ tbsp caraway seeds

1. Cut off the rinds of the cheese. Grate the cheese into a bowl. Mix in the rest of the ingredients.

2. Stir carefully until it becomes a smooth paste.

3. Fill a pretty jar with the half hardened paste. Cover with a lid and let the krukost stand and mature in the fridge for 1–2 weeks.

CHEESE AND CHRISTMAS BELONG TOGETHER

Since time immemorial, revelers have set out the best local cheeses with the other delicacies on the Christmas table. A cheese tray at Christmas doesn't have to consist of many varieties. Perhaps a yellow, a bleu, and a creamy cheese. Choose your own favorites. Stilton and cheddar are two Christmas classics and cream cheese, herb cheese, Västerbotten cheese, and bleu cheese are delicious varieties in our home county of Sweden. Other good options are extra aged hard cheeses and artisanal cheeses of all varieties.

On Christmas Eve in Sweden, we eat a hodgepodge of dishes, and therefore food on Christmas Day can be delicious and traditional with clean, elegant flavors and festive sides. In many other countries, Christmas Day is the highlight of the holidays, so we'd love for you to prepare a glorious dinner with turkey, fish, or duck.

Christmas Day

GLORIA IN EXCELSIS DEO

God Jul Gott Nytt År   önskar
                            Elisabeth

Lutefisk

A fantastic and unique dish that divides Sweden between those who politely refrain and those who love it. Lutefisk can calm the most unsettled stomach, since it is so alkaline.

8 PORTIONS

6½–9 lbs (3–4 kg) lutefisk
1–1½ tbsp salt
FOR SERVING:
béchamel sauce (see recipe to the right)
freshly ground allspice
freshly ground black pepper
Swedish and Skånsk mustard (or spicy brown mustard)
boiled peas or soy beans
diced fried pork, optional

1. Place the fish in water to soak for a few hours.

2. Heat the oven to 400°F (200°C). Place the fish the skin-side down in an ovenproof dish or long baking sheet. Sprinkle with salt. Cover the with parchment paper or aluminum foil.

3. Place the pan in the oven and let the lutefisk cook for 40–50 minutes. Remove the liquid that's formed after about half the cooking time. Drain the liquid once again just before serving.

4. Serve with béchamel sauce (see recipe to the right), allspice, black pepper, Swedish and Skånsk mustard, and boiled peas or soy beans. Norwegian style Lutefisk is also tasty with diced fried pork.

Béchamel sauce

A classic white sauce is not to be scoffed at. Wonderful with lutefisk and its accompaniments.

4 PORTIONS

5 tbsp butter
4 tbsp wheat flour
1 quart (1 liter) whole milk
1 bay leaf
½–¾ tsp salt
freshly ground white pepper
freshly grated nutmeg

1. Heat the butter in a pot. Add the wheat flour and let it sizzle for about 1 minute without letting it brown. Pour in the milk a little at a time while stirring. Add the bay leaf.

2. Let the sauce simmer while stirring for 4 minutes. Add salt, pepper, and nutmeg to taste.

Béchamel sauce with finesse

A few drops of truffle oil and a couple of chopped boiled eggs transforms the béchamel sauce into something more elegant and unique.

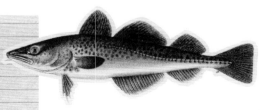

If not everyone likes lutefisk, you can boil or bake a bit of cod and serve it together. That way everyone can get something to their taste.

Poached salmon or pike

The old method of poaching fish gives a very nice flavor and texture. The important thing is to not boil the fish for too long or else it dries out.

8–12 SMALL PORTIONS

**1 whole fish, for example salmon or pike
(3–5½ lbs / 1½–2 kg)**
STOCK:
1 red onion
1 carrot
4 cups (1 liter) water
1 lemon, juice
4 tbsp white vinegar (12%)
3 bay leaves
10 white peppercorns
10 black peppercorns
some sprigs of dill
½ tsp dill seeds
4 tbsp salt
FOR GARNISH:
½ cucumber
3 boiled eggs
mayonnaise
dill sprigs

1. Peel and roughly slice the red onion. Peel and slice the carrot.

2. Place all the ingredients for the stock in an oblong or round fish pot, and bring to a boil.

3. Clean the salmon (and gut it if it wasn't done in the store). Cut away the gills and fins. Rinse the fish.

4. Put the fish in the stock and let it slowly simmer for 30 minutes. The water should only barely be moving, it should not be bubbling. Skim off the foam as needed. Try to see if the fish is done by feeling whether the meat is coming off the backbone.

5. Remove the skin from the fish and let it cool in the stock.

6. Remove the fish from the stock and place on a tray. Garnish with sliced cucumber, sliced eggs, mayonnaise, dill and lemon slices. Radishes, fish roe, and cooked white asparagus are other alternatives. Set aside to cool. Serve with the horseradish cream to the right.

Fish in jelly

If you want the fish in jelly, then dissolve 2 gelatin leaves in the warm stock and brush the salmon with the mixture.

Horseradish cream

You can replace the horseradish with mustard or wasabi if you like.

8–12 SMALL PORTIONS

1¼ cups (300 ml) crème fraiche or sour cream
3 tbsp freshly grated horseradish
salt to taste

1. Mix all the ingredients. Ideally, let the cream stand for a while so the flavors develop.

2. Season to taste.

Karoline's oven-baked salmon
with gremolata

A simple salmon dish that ends up perfectly juicy every single time!

4–6 PORTIONS

approx. 2¼ lbs (1 kg) side of salmon
3 tbsp olive oil
3 tbsp melted butter
salt
pepper
GREMOLATA:
2 lemons
3 garlic cloves
½ cup (100 ml) chopped flat leaf parsley

1. Preheat the oven to 250°F (120°C).

2. Grease an oven dish and add a little salt and pepper.

3. Place the salmon in the dish, pour the olive oil and the melted butter on top. Season with salt and pepper.

4. Place the salmon in the oven and bake for about 35 minutes. Carefully check the center of the salmon to see if the liquid runs clear or use a digital kitchen thermometer to see if the inner temperature is 130°F (54°C).

5. Rinse the lemons and grate the outermost layer of the peel. Finely chop the garlic. Mix the lemon peel with garlic and flat leaf parsley. Sprinkle the gremolata on the salmon. Serve with mashed potatoes or rice.

Baked stuffed salmon

An elegant dish that looks more difficult than it is.

6−8 PORTIONS

1 side of salmon with skin (approx. 2½ lbs / 1¼ kg)
approx. 1 tbsp salt
STUFFING:
2 egg whites
1 cup (250 ml) whipping cream
1 tbsp Dijon mustard
1 tbsp freshly grated horseradish
¼ cup (50 ml) finely chopped dill
freshly ground black pepper
1 tsp salt
FOR GARNISH:
dill sprigs
lemon slices

1. Cut away the wide middle part of the side of salmon, skin and all. The piece should consist of about 2/3 of the entire side. Add salt.

2. Cut off the skin from the rest of the meat and chop the meat fairly finely (or mix it quickly in a food processor).

3. Combine the chopped salmon and all the other stuffing ingredients, but add one egg white at a time.

4. Preheat the oven to 400°F (200°C). Place the side of the salmon in a greased baking sheet (or other oven dish). Cover with the stuffing.

5. Place the salmon in the oven and bake for 15 minutes.

6. Turn off the oven and let the salmon sit another 20−25 minutes until the fish and the stuffing are cooked, but not dry.

7. Serve the salmon hot or lukewarm. Garnish with dill and lemon slices.

Luxurious fish soup
with gremolata

A delicious fish soup with winter flavors. Serve with a dollop of crème fraiche or add whipping cream for a creamier soup.

8 PORTIONS

14 oz (400 g) fresh salmon
10½ oz (300 g) fresh pike-perch fillet
1 onion
1 garlic clove
1 head of fennel
1 carrot
½ celeriac
1 tbsp olive oil
1 tsp fennel seeds
2−3 star anise
½ g saffron, optional
¾ cup (200 ml) dry white wine
4¼ cups (1 liter) fish bouillon (4½ cups of water and 2 fish bouillon cubes or readymade fish stock—ask at the store!)
¾ cup (200 ml) whipping cream, optional
10−20 cherry tomatoes
⅔ lb (300 g) peeled shrimp
salt and pepper
GREMOLATA:
3 tbsp finely chopped flat leaf parsley
1 garlic clove, minced
1 tsp lemon zest

1. Cut the fish fillets into large cubes and set aside. Peel and mince the onion and garlic. Peel and cut all vegetables into thin slices or strips.

2. Heat the oil over medium heat and fry the onion until soft. Add the fennel seeds and star anise. Stir well. Add all the finely cut vegetables and fry for a few minutes.

3. Add the wine and bouillon and let it all boil.

4. If you want a creamier soup add ¾ cup (200 ml) cream and let the soup simmer for another couple of minutes.

5. Add the tomatoes and fish cubes and let simmer for 2−3 minutes.

6. Mix the ingredients for the gremolata in a small bowl.

7. Add in the shrimp when serving. Season with salt and pepper. Serve with the gremolata and preferably some crème fraiche and delicious bread just out of the oven.

Christmas turkey

Standing up and carving an enormous turkey feels like a bit of a cliché—but maybe not at Christmas! There are countless ways too cook this holiday bird. The trick is to get it juicy and flavorful with a crispy skin. Check out the tips on the next page and good luck!

8–10 PORTIONS

approx. 11 lbs (5 kg) whole turkey
1 orange, wedged
a couple of sprigs of rosemary
olive oil
salt and pepper
2 onions
2 carrots
2 celery stalks
STUFFING:
2 onions
olive oil
3–4 leaves of fresh sage
a pinch of nutmeg
salt and freshly ground pepper
⅔ lb (300 g) ground pork
¼ cup (50 ml) dried cranberries (or finely chopped apricots)
1 lemon, zest
¼ cup (50 ml) breadcrumbs or panko

1. The turkey should be room temperature, so follow the directions on the packaging to thaw and warm it safely. Rinse the turkey and pat it dry with kitchen towels. Add salt and pepper and rub that into the skin.

2. Preheat the oven to 450°F (225°C).

3. Peel and chop the onion for the stuffing and fry it in olive oil until soft. Add sage, nutmeg, salt, and pepper and fry for another minute.

4. Place the onion in a bowl and let it cool a bit. Add the ground pork, cranberries, lemon zest, and breadcrumbs and mix it by hand.

5. Stick half of the stuffing in the turkey's neck hole. Don't pack it in too hard. Then put the rest of the stuffing in the stomach cavity, with the orange wedges and rosemary.

6. Peel and roughly chop another two onions, the carrot, and celery and put in a large baking dish. Put the bird on top of the vegetables and cover with foil. Place in the oven and reduce the heat to 350°F (180°C).

7. Calculate that the turkey will need to sit in the oven for 30–40 minutes for every 2¼ lbs (per kg), so an 11 lb (5 kg) turkey needs about 3 hours in the oven. But be sure to read the directions on the packaging.

8. Remove the foil and baste the turkey with the drippings when about 45 minutes remain. Check that the turkey is done by sticking a knife into the thickest part of the leg. The juice should run clear. Or use a digital kitchen thermometer. The turkey should have an inner temperature of 160°F (70°C).

9. Let the turkey rest for about 30 minutes, covered in foil and a kitchen towel before carving.

10. We'd love for you to use the pan drippings to make gravy to serve with the turkey. Skim away the foam and put the whole tray on a warm stove. Stir in a couple of tablespoons of flour and about 4½ cups (1 liter) chicken broth and whisk until it thickens. Strain.

11. Serve the turkey with the gravy, hasselback potatoes (see recipe below), and boiled Brussels sprouts.

Hasselback potatoes

A classic where we use extra fluffy breadcrumbs and a little sea salt to strengthen the crispiness. If you want to add flavor to the potatoes, you can sprinkle 1 tsp caraway seeds at the same time as you sprinkle on the breadcrumbs and the salt.

4 PORTIONS

8–12 firm potatoes
3 tbsp butter
½ tsp salt
2 tbsp breadcrumbs, preferably panko
1 tsp sea salt (or 2–3 tbsp aged hard cheese)

1. Peel and rinse the potatoes. Make thin slices in each potato, but don't cut all the way through; they should still be connected at the bottom.

2. Preheat the oven to 450°F (225°C).

3. Melt the butter in an ovenproof dish or a small baking sheet and place the potatoes there, sliced-side up.

4. Brush the potatoes with the melted butter and add salt. Fry in the oven for about 30 minutes. Sprinkle with breadcrumbs and sea salt and fry for another 10–15 minutes.

WHEN YOU'RE ABOUT TO COOK TURKEY

The turkey should be at room temperature when you place it in the oven. A frozen turkey that weighs 11 lbs (5 kg) thaws in about 24 hours at room temperature and in 60–70 hours in the fridge.

Don't pack in the stuffing too tight, since it can affect the cooking time. If you don't want to have a classic stuffing, you can also stuff the turkey with, for example, 1 sliced orange, 1 wedged onion, and a couple of sprigs of rosemary. Or roughly chopped apples and prunes.

It takes time to cook a turkey! Make sure you get started well in advance of the dinner, since the turkey needs many hours in the oven. It should be cooked through by the time you serve it.

To baste or not to baste? There are different theories about basting, so do what you think best. Some believe that the oven temperature drops when you open the oven and that this is what makes a juicier turkey—not the basting itself.

Duck breast
with blackcurrant or lingonberries

Canard au cassis—duck with blackcurrant sauce—is the French classic that inspired this elegant dish.

4 PORTIONS

2–3 duck breasts (approx. 1¼ lb / 600 g)
¼ cup (50 ml) finely chopped flat leaf parsley
¾ cup (200 ml) berries, preferably blackcurrants or lingonberries
salt
freshly ground black pepper
fresh berries for garnish
BERRY SAUCE:
2 tbsp butter
½ onion, finely chopped
1 tbsp wheat flour
2 cups (500 ml) chicken stock (1 bouillon cube + water)
½ cup (100 ml) blackcurrants or other berries
1 bay leaf
½ cup (100 ml) full-bodied red wine
salt
freshly ground black pepper

1. Clean the berries and rinse if necessary.

2. Salt and pepper the duck breast.

3. Preheat the oven to 150°F (70°C). Fry the duck breast in a frying pan—first the skin side and then the meat side. Place the duck breasts on a baking sheet and place in oven. Save the fat in a small bowl. If you want, you can stick in a digital kitchen thermometer and set it to 140°F (60°C).

4. Prepare the sauce while the duck is in the oven. Melt the butter in a pot and fry the chopped onions for a while, but don't let them brown. Sprinkle in the flour, stir, and let fry for a minute. Add the bouillon and berries, bay leaf, and wine. Add salt and pepper. Let it all simmer for 20 minutes.

5. Strain the sauce and then pour back into the pot. Let it simmer to just the right thickness. Add salt and pepper to taste.

6. Remove the duck breast when the core temperature reaches 140°F (60°C). Let rest for 5 minutes.

7. Slice the duck breast diagonally into thin slices and place on a warm serving tray. Pour the sauce all around. Garnish with parsley and/or fresh berries and serve with diced potatoes fried in the duck fat, or with mashed potatoes. The duck breast can also be served whole to be carved at the table.

Saffron pilaf

A lovely saffron pilaf with spices and a hint of sweetness from dried fruit goes perfectly with the Christmas meats. You can easily double the recipe for a large family dinner.

4 PORTIONS

approx. ¼ cup (50 ml) blanched and peeled almonds (see p. 57)
9 oz (250 g) basmati rice
2 shallots
2 tbsp olive oil
3 whole cardamom pods or ½ tsp lightly crushed cardamom seeds
1 g saffron (2 envelopes)
½ tsp salt
1¼ cups (300 ml) water
1 tbsp currants or finely chopped dried cranberries
1 tbsp butter
1–2 tbsp finely chopped cilantro

1. Place the almonds on a baking sheet. Place the baking sheet in the oven, and heat the oven to 300°F (150°C). Let it stand for 15 minutes or until the oven is warm and the almonds smell lovely.

2. Rinse the rice in cold water. Chop the onion finely.

3. Fry the finely chopped onions in a pot with oil until they are soft and transparent. Add rice, cardamom, and half the saffron and stir until all the rice is shiny with oil. Add salt and water. Finally stir in the currants or dried cranberries. Cover and let simmer for 15 minutes or until the rice is done.

4. Stir in the butter and the rest of the saffron. Serve with almonds and fresh cilantro.

Gott Nytt År

A Happy New

Season's Greetings

WITH BEST WISHES

FOR A

HAPPY

NEW

YEAR

New Year's

The month of December is coming to an end and we've saved some of the most delicious dishes for last. Celebrate the new year with crisp flavors and lighter food. Choose shellfish, the finest meats, and an extra luxurious dessert. If you're hosting a big party, lobster and shellfish for all can get a bit pricey, in which case, a lobster salad is a fantastic alternative. Or you could always do a potluck and let the guests contribute! Happy New Year!

Lobster salad

If you need one lobster to feed many, then this salad is perfect. Citrus and lobster go very well together and if you make the effort to fillet the oranges, it will feel that much fancier.

4 APPETIZER PORTIONS

2 large red onions
½ pomegranate
2 oranges
1 avocado
¼ cup (50 ml) olive oil
1 lemon, juice
sea salt and freshly ground black pepper
1 cooked lobster
arugula lettuce

1. Peel and finely chop the onion. Seed the pomegranate (see p. 118). Fillet the oranges by first cutting away the peel and the pith, and then cut out the wedges with a sharp knife. Cut the avocado in half, remove the pit and dice the flesh. Toss the ingredients in a bowl.

2. Mix the olive oil, lemon juice, salt, and pepper. Season to taste. Drizzle the dressing over the ingredients in the bowl and toss well. Set aside.

3. Cut the lobster down the middle and carefully pick out all the meat. Don't forget the claws! Cut the meat into strips.

4. Add the lobster meat to the bowl and let it all stand in the fridge for an hour or so.

5. Serve on a bed of arugula.

Oysters
with grapefruit and chili

This appetizer with its ocean fresh, hot, and lovely flavor will perk you up.

6 PORTIONS

6 oysters
1 white grapefruit
1 pink grapefruit
1 mild red chili
freshly ground black pepper
2–3 tbsp olive oil, preferably a fruity variety

1. Begin by cutting away the grapefruit peels with a sharp knife. Then, cut the grapefruit into thin slices and the slices into smaller pieces. You can also fillet the grapefruit (see p. 146). Place the grapefruit and all the juice in a bowl.

2. Cut the chili in half, seed it, and finely chop it. Chop it until it becomes mushy and juicy. Mix it with the grapefruit in the bowl.

3. Open the oysters (see p. 172). Pour all the oyster liquid into the bowl with the grapefruit and chili. Add freshly ground pepper to taste and distribute it across the oysters. Drizzle with olive oil and serve immediately.

Lobster in butter bouillon

A luxurious starter that warms you up.

4 PORTIONS

2 cooked lobsters
2 cups (500 ml) water
¾ cup (200 ml) dry white wine
½ onion, finely chopped
4¼ cups (1 liter) shellfish broth (water + concentrated lobster broth)
a pinch of saffron
5⅓ oz (150 g) Savoy cabbage
2 oz (50 g) green asparagus or haricots verts
6–8 radishes
1 tbsp finely chopped fresh chervil or parsley
1 tbsp freshly squeezed lemon juice
3½ tbsp (50 g) butter

1. Cut the lobsters in half and remove all the meat carefully. Cut the meat into smaller pieces and set aside.

2. Chop or lightly crush all the shells and heads and place them in the water and wine with the chopped onions. Bring to a boil and simmer for about 20 minutes. Strain the bouillon into a new pot, return to a boil, and let it cook uncovered until ½ cup (100 ml) remains.

3. Pour the shellfish broth into 2 cups (500 ml) boiled water and add saffron. Bring to a boil and simmer uncovered for about 10 minutes.

4. Clean the vegetables: cut the Savoy cabbage into strips and the asparagus into smaller pieces, divide the radishes. Cut off the chervil or parsley stems. At this stage the bouillon can be made in advance.

5. Bring the bouillon to a boil just before serving. Add the vegetables and cook for 2–3 minutes. Add the lemon juice and add lobster. Remove from the heat and stir in the butter so it melts. Pour into a large bowl or into 4 small bowls. Sprinkle the herbs on top and serve.

Shellfish buffet

A lot of seafood is at its best during the winter. Choose your favorites. Oysters are conveniently opened with a special oyster knife—handle with care.

4 PORTIONS

a choice of delicious shellfish, for example:
2 cooked lobsters or 1 cooked crab
8 cooked Norway lobsters
12 oysters or 1 lb (500 g) unpeeled shrimp

1. Cut the lobsters in half. Open the oysters (see below). Arrange all the shellfish on a serving tray, possibly on a bed of ice.

2. Set out some delicious sauces, for example avocado mayonnaise, sesame dressing, and red onion yogurt (see the following recipes), and lemon, salt, pepper, Worcestershire sauce, and preferably some white bread.

Avocado mayonnaise

Don't make this sauce more than two hours before serving. It goes brown quite quickly.

4 SMALL PORTIONS

1 avocado
½ green chili
⅔ cup (150 ml) mayonnaise
1 tbsp freshly squeezed lemon juice
black pepper
salt to taste

1. Remove the pit from the avocado. Scoop out the flesh whole and cut into pieces.

2. Cut the chili and seed it, roughly chop it, and mix it with the avocado, mayonnaise, and lemon into a smooth cream. Add salt and pepper to taste.

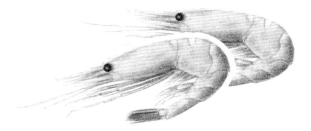

Sesame dressing

A dressing inspired by Japanese cuisine.

4 PORTIONS

½ cup (100 ml) Japanese soy sauce
4 tbsp freshly squeezed lemon juice
2 tsp sesame oil
2 tsp roasted sesame seeds

1. Mix all the ingredients. Add more soy sauce or lemon according to taste.

Red onion yogurt

The tahini gives this dipping sauce a smooth and mild character.

4 PORTIONS

2 cups (500 ml) thick yogurt
1 finely chopped red onion
2–3 garlic cloves, minced
1 tbsp tahini (sesame paste)
½ tsp salt

1. Mix all the ingredients in a bowl.

2. Let the sauce stand in the fridge for an hour so the flavors can develop. Add salt and tahini to taste. Serve the sauce cold.

HOW TO OPEN OYSTERS

1. Place the oyster on a table with the curved side down. Place your hand over the oyster, with a towel in between for protection in case you slip.

2. Use an oyster knife or a thin knife and push in the blade (which shouldn't be too short) just by the joint. Wiggle the knife until you hear a small click. Then, push the knife in a little further and cut off the muscle.

Russian blinis

with mushroom salad and trout roe

Lovely, fluffy blinis served with a Finnish-Russian mushroom salad.

8 BLINIS

¼ pack of fresh yeast (12 g)
½ tsp granulated sugar
1 cup (225 ml) water
½ cup (100 ml) whole milk
1 egg yolk
½ tsp salt
⅔ cup (150 ml) wheat flour
1 egg white
1 tbsp Canola oil + 1 tbsp butter
TOPPING:
3½ oz (100 g) trout roe
mushroom salad (see next recipe)
a few sprigs of dill

1. If you like, prepare the mushroom salad a day in advance (see next recipe). Let the roe drain in a coffee filter in the fridge for a couple of hours (to firm up).

2. Stir the yeast and sugar in tepid, 99°F (37°C) water and let rise for 20 minutes beneath a kitchen towel.

3. Heat the milk to 99°F (37°C). Combine the egg yolk, milk, and salt in a spacious bowl. Stir in the yeast mixture and the wheat flour. Stir into a smooth, thick batter. Let rise for about 3 hours.

4. Whisk the egg white into a stiff foam and fold it into the paste.

5. Cook the blinis carefully in oil and butter over medium heat in a griddle or frying pan. Use 1–2 tbsp batter for each blini. Flip the blinis when they've risen and the surface is solid.

6. Serve the blinis warm and topped with mushroom salad, roe, and a sprig of dill.

Mushroom salad

A salad inspired by Russian and Finnish cooking.

8 PORTIONS

¾ cup (200 ml) cream or sour cream
¾ cup (200 ml) wild mushrooms (or ¼ cup (50 ml) dried wild mushrooms)
1 tbsp butter
plenty of sea salt
2 tbsp finely chopped dill
½ onion, finely chopped
a couple of drops of lemon juice

1. Pour the cream or sour cream into a coffee filter or a strainer and let drain in the fridge for 2–3 hours.

2. Fry the mushrooms in butter over medium heat until they take on a little color. Stir every so often. Remove the frying pan from the heat and let the mushrooms cool.

3. In a bowl, mix the fried mushrooms with salt, dill, and the drained sour cream.

4. Stir in the chopped onion. Add salt and lemon to taste. Ideally, prepare the salad a day in advance, otherwise it needs to stand in the fridge for a while.

Tagliata

A luxury dinner in no time! A piece of thinly sliced beef tenderloin is also perfect to serve buffet-style.

4–6 PORTIONS

approx. 14 oz (400 g) beef tenderloin (2.5–3.5 oz (75–100 g) per person)
1 sprig of fresh rosemary
1 tsp dried or 1 tbsp fresh oregano
½ tsp freshly grated black pepper
1 tsp sea salt
1 bunch of arugula (2½ oz / 70 g)
a couple of cherry tomatoes
2–3 tbsp olive oil
½ lemon

1. Purchase the most evenly sized tenderloin possible. Remove the meat from the fridge about half an hour before you're ready to cook it.

2. Chop the rosemary and place it and the other spices and salt on a small tray or cutting board. Roll the meat in the spices; press down a bit so they stick properly.

3. Heat a grill pan over high heat. Grill the tenderloin for about 5 minutes. Flip the meat when it starts to brown.

4. Wrap the grilled meat in aluminum foil and let it stand for about 5 minutes.

5. Cut the meat in thin slices. Arrange them wrapped on a serving tray. Add arugula and halved cherry tomatoes. Drizzle with olive oil, squeeze some lemon juice on top, and add a little salt and pepper. Serve immediately.

New Year's punch

A festive, refreshing, and vibrant red punch to ring in the New Year. You can even freeze pomegranate seeds into the ice cubes.

8–10 GLASSES

4¼ cups (1 liter) pomegranate juice
½ cup (100 ml) Cointreau
the seeds from ½ pomegranate
ice
2 cups (½ liter) apple or pear cider
1 bottle Champagne or dry white sparkling wine
thin slices of orange and lime

1. Combine the pomegranate juice and the Cointreau in a large punch bowl. Add the pomegranate seeds and ice.

2. Pour in the cider and Champagne. Add the orange and lime slices and serve immediately.

Baked fillet of reindeer
with bleu cheese

This is a perfect party dish, and it can easily be prepared beforehand. If you don't live in a place where reindeer meat is readily available, you can use venison instead. Serve with potatoes, or, for best results, add a red wine sauce.

4 PORTIONS

1 lb (425 g) reindeer fillet or venison fillet
salt
1 tbsp butter + 1 tbsp Canola oil
freshly ground black pepper
freshly ground white pepper
STEW:
¾ cup (200 ml) whipping cream
7 oz (200 g) bleu cheese
black pepper
PASTRY:
1 packet of frozen puff pastry (approx. 14 oz / 400 g)
1 whisked egg yolk

1. Clean away any sinews, membranes, and large pieces of fat from the fillet. Salt the meat on all sides and let stand for 15 minutes so the salt sinks in a bit (you can do this in advance; the meat won't become dry).

2. Fry the meat on all sides in butter and oil in a frying pan or a large pot (the more carefully you fry, the stronger the flavor—you can even gladly save the juices to add to a red wine sauce). Pepper the meat carefully and let cool.

3. Heat the cream and crumble in the cheese. Stir until it becomes a thick and fairly smooth cream. Add pepper.

4. Preheat the oven to 400°F (200°C). Thaw the puff pastry sheets. Roll the sheets into a rectangle, roughly 8 x 16 in (20 x 40 cm).

5. Spread a third of the cheese cream onto the dough. Place the fillet on top and cover it with the rest of the cheese cream. Fold the dough around the meat and brush with the egg yolk to "glue" the edges together. Place it all on a baking sheet without a rim.

6. Brush the dough with the rest of the egg yolk and place the tray on the lowest rack in the oven. Bake for about 15 minutes (until the inner temperature is around 130°F / 55°C —use a digital kitchen thermometer). Remove the meat from the oven and let it rest, covered, for at least 5 minutes.

7. Slice the meat and serve with red wine sauce (see following recipe) and hasselback potatoes (see p. 164), or potato wedges. Edamame beans or haricots verts are good accompaniments.

Red wine sauce

A red wine sauce is the perfect addition to a delicious piece of meat. If the red wine is delicious and the onion and carrot are fresh, making the sauce is simple. If you like, you can thicken the sauce by sprinkling the onion and carrots with flour before pouring in the red wine, or stir a mixture of cornstarch and water into the sauce before it is heated for the last time.

4 PORTIONS

3 shallots or 1 onion
3 crushed garlic cloves
1 small carrot, diced
1 tbsp olive oil + 1 tbsp butter
2 tsp wheat flour or 1 tbsp cornstarch, optional
1 cup (250 ml) of a soft and full-bodied red wine
2 cups (½ liter) dark beef stock (water + bouillon cube)
2 tsp tomato purée
1 bay leaf
1 sprig of fresh rosemary or ½ tsp dried
1 spring of fresh thyme or ½ tsp dried
¼ tsp cayenne pepper
3½ tbsp (50 g) butter
salt to taste
freshly ground black pepper
a few drops of lemon juice

1. Fry onion, garlic, and carrot in olive oil and butter in a thick bottomed, preferably wide, pot. Stir and sizzle until the onion and carrot soften and smell lovely. Sprinkle in the wheat flour if you choose this option.

2. Pour in the red wine, stock, tomato purée, bay leaf, rosemary, thyme, and cayenne pepper. Let simmer uncovered for about 20 minutes. Add more water if needed.

3. Strain the sauce. Stir in the butter. Add salt and pepper to taste and a few drops of lemon juice. Serve.

Beetroot salad

Sweet beetroots in a refreshing dressing.

4–6 SMALL PORTIONS

6 normal sized fresh beetroots (1⅓–1½ lbs / 600–700 g)
8½ cups (2 liters) water + 1 tsp salt
2 tbsp finely chopped parsley
DRESSING:
1 tbsp lemon juice
1 tbsp olive oil
salt to taste
freshly ground black pepper

1. Brush the beetroots and boil them in the water and salt for 40–60 minutes. They should be soft but not mushy. Drain the water and let them steam in a colander. Rub off the skin with your hands.

2. Cut the beetroots into wedges, or dice them.

3. Mix the dressing in a spacious bowl. Fold the beetroots into it. Sprinkle with parsley and serve.

Babaganoush

A classic Lebanese mixture with a delightful flavor.

4–6 SMALL PORTIONS

3–4 eggplants
3 garlic cloves, minced
approx. 1 tsp salt
½ cup (100 ml) tahini (sesame paste)
4 tbsp lemon juice
½ tsp ground cumin
2 tbsp fruity olive oil
a few black olives or pomegranate seeds

1. Cut the egglants in half lengthwise and salt the flesh on both sides. Let stand for 30 minutes.

2. Rinse the salt from the eggplants and then grill them slowly in a grill pan until they're soft and have attained a nice surface. Pull off the skin and save any juice that might come out.

3. Dice the eggplant flesh and mix with the garlic, salt, tahini, lemon juice, and cumin into an even mixture. Let stand in the fridge for at least 1 hour.

4. Place the mixture in a bowl, make a small dent in the middle, and pour in the olive oil. Decorate with black olives or pomegranate seeds.

Green hummus

Inexpensive and quick to mix together. The leftovers can be used as a healthy "butter" for your sandwiches as you enter the New Year with your healthy resolutions.

6–8 PORTIONS

1 can of chickpeas (14 oz/400 g)
½ tsp salt
1–2 tbsp freshly squeezed lemon juice
2 tbsp finely chopped flat leaf parsley
1 garlic clove, finely chopped
2 tbsp tahini (sesame paste)
a pinch of cumin
2 tbsp olive oil

1. Drain the chickpeas in a colander and rinse them in cold water. Remove 5–6 chickpeas and put the rest in a food processor. Add salt, 1 tbsp lemon juice, leaf parsley, and garlic and mix it all into an even paste. Or mix it all with an immersion blender.

2. Stir in the tahini and add lemon and cumin to taste.

3. Place in a bowl, make a small dent in the middle, and place in the extra chickpeas. Pour in the olive oil.

Fried chicken wings
or drumsticks

These slightly tangy and just spicy enough chicken wings are common on the Lebanese mezze table. If you can't find wings just use drumsticks instead.

4–6 PORTIONS

approx. 2 lbs (900 g) chicken wings or drumsticks
4 tbsp olive oil
2 tsp salt
approx. ¼ tsp black pepper
½ tsp paprika powder
3 garlic cloves
approx. 4 tbsp lemon juice
2 tbsp chopped fresh cilantro

1. Preheat the oven to 450°F (225°C).

2. Mix olive oil, salt, pepper, and paprika in a deep bowl. Press or mince the garlic and add it to the bowl. Add the chicken and toss well. Pour onto baking sheet.

3. Place the sheet in the oven and bake the wings for 20 minutes, or the drumsticks for 35 minutes. Check on the chicken every now and then and turn the pieces with tongs.

4. Mix the lemon juice and cilantro.

5. Remove the baking sheet from the oven and pour the lemon and cilantro mix over the chicken. Return to the oven and cook for another 3–5 minutes. Set the oven to broil if you think the chicken looks pale. Serve hot or room temperature.

Falafel

A simple and easy falafel recipe. You can vary the seasoning with thyme, ground ginger, and paprika.

4–6 PORTIONS

2 cans boiled chickpeas (each 14 oz / 400 g)
2 garlic cloves
½ cup (100 ml) parsley sprigs
2 tsp ground cumin
2 tsp ground whole coriander
½ tsp ground cinnamon
½ tsp harissa
4 tbsp wheat flour
salt to taste
¼ cup (50 ml) Canola oil
¾ cup (200 ml) sesame seeds

1. Rinse the chickpeas and let them drain. Mix the garlic, parsley, cumin, coriander, cinnamon, harissa, flour, and salt into a fairly smooth mixture. Taste and adjust seasoning.

2. With your wet hands, form 20 "meatballs" from of the paste. Roll them in sesame seeds.

3. Heat the oil in a large frying pan and fry the falafel on all sides for about 5 minutes. Serve with tomato sauce or mint yogurt and fried or toasted pita bread.

Fattoush

This is a more unusual green salad. It's spicy, and has a unique texture because it contains toasted pita bread. The sumac spice can be bought in Asian grocery stores.

4–6 SMALL PORTIONS

1 pita bread
2 cups (500 ml) oil for deep frying
¼ cucumber
½ red, ½ yellow, and ½ green bell pepper
5 radishes
2 sprigs of fresh mint
2 tbsp chopped flat leaf parsley
4 romaine lettuce leaves
DRESSING:
3 garlic cloves
½ tsp dried mint
½ tsp salt
½ tsp paprika powder
½ tsp sumac
¾ cup (175 ml) lemon juice
1–2 tbsp olive oil

1. Cut the pita bread and separate so you have two thin halves. Deep fry the bread in oil at 350°F (180°C) until it is golden brown. Measure the temperature with a digital kitchen thermometer. You can also toast the bread at 400°F (200°C) for about 10 minutes.

2. Crush the bread or cut it into strips and let cool.

3. Cut the cucumber lengthwise, seed it with a small spoon, and slice it. Cut the paprika into rough strips and slice the radishes. Roughly chop mint, leaf parsley, and lettuce. Place all of it in a salad bowl.

4. Press the garlic and mix the ingredients for the dressing in a separate bowl. Drizzle over the salad. Mix and garnish with bread just before serving, so it doesn't get soggy.

LUXURIOUS AND SIMPLE

A festive and luxurious New Year's dessert is to serve a simple fruit salad or sorbet in tall glasses and pour in chilled sparkling wine or Champagne just before serving.

Frosted fruit

The most beautiful centerpiece is also a dessert.

4–6 PORTIONS

beautiful fruit and berries, for example small red apples, grapes, peeled tangerines, and/or fresh figs
1–2 whisked egg whites
½–1⅓ cups (100–300 ml) granulated sugar
1 red rose, optional

1. Brush the fruit, berries, and the rose (optional) with the lightly whisked egg white and dip them in the granulated sugar.

2. Let harden for a couple of hours and add more sugar if required.

Zabaglione

A classic dessert sauce or cream and a luxurious finale to a delicious meal. The zabaglione must be made while the guests wait, unless you mix in a little whipped cream. In that case, it becomes a Marsala-scented vanilla cream, and it can be left in the fridge for a short while should you wish to prepare the dessert in advance.

4–6 PORTIONS

7 oz (200 g) frozen berries, for example, raspberries, blueberries, or blackberries
3 egg yolks
¼ cup (50 ml) granulated sugar
¼ cup (50 ml) Marsala wine
1 tsp lightly crushed cardamom

1. Let the berries thaw. Whisk the egg yolks and sugar until white and fluffy in a stainless steel bowl. Carefully whisk in the marsala wine and cardamom.

2. Place the bowl in a water bath over a pot with simmering water. Whisk for 5–10 minutes with an handheld mixer until the sauce thickens and froths.

3. Put the berries in tall glasses. Spoon the zabaglione on top. Serve with sweet biscuits or gingerbread cookies (see p. 71).

GLASS VASE LANTERNS

An everyday glass vase can easily become an ornate lantern with a little help from egg whites and sugar.

You need: Glass vases in different sizes, 1 egg white, a couple of tablespoons of granulated sugar, paper stencils, brush.

Cut the paper into the shapes you want.

Lightly whisk the egg white with a fork.

Stick the paper stencils on the inside of the vase where you want your pattern.

Using a brush, trace the egg white along the pattern on the outside of the vase and immediately sprinkle sugar on top.

Let it stand and harden properly before removing the stencil.

Molten chocolate cake

A luxurious and creamy dark chocolate fondant. Remember to serve it immediately after it comes out of the oven.

8–10 PORTIONS

4½ oz (125 g) dark chocolate (minumum 70%)
½ cup (125 g) butter
4 eggs
¾ cup (200 ml) powdered sugar
2 tbsp Cointreau or rum
⅓ cup (75 ml) wheat flour
cocoa or wheat flour for the pan
FOR SERVING:
cocoa powder, optional
vanilla ice cream or whipped cream
raspberries

1. Put the chocolate and butter in a bowl that can withstand heat. Melt them in a water bath. You can also use a microwave.

2. Whisk the egg and sugar into a fluffy foam. Stir it into the melted chocolate. Pour in Cointreau or rum and finally fold in the flour (you can even sift the flour into the batter). Let the batter stand in the fridge overnight or for at least 2 hours.

3. Preheat the oven to 400°F (200°C).

4. Grease a muffin pan or similar. Sprinkle with a little flour or cocoa powder.

5. Fill ¾ of the way with batter. Bake the cakes in the oven for 8–10 minutes—watch them carefully the whole time. The surface should be solid but the center should still be runny. They should jiggle a bit when the tray is wobbled.

6. Carefully loosen along the edges of the cakes with a thin spatula or knife and lift them out of the pans. The key is to be very careful so they don't break and the contents spills out too soon!

7. If you like, sift some cocoa powder on top and serve immediately with soft vanilla ice cream or whipped cream and raspberry sauce.

Lime fromage

This fromage is easiest to make in pans. Serve cold, preferably with a slice of peeled lime that has been candied on both sides.

4–6 PORTIONS

5 sheets of gelatin
3 eggs
2 egg yolks
⅔ cup (150 ml) granulated sugar
2 limes, zest
5–6 limes, juice
1 lime for garnish
1 cup (250 ml) whipping cream

1. Place the gelatin sheets in cold water for 5 minutes.

2. Stir together the whole eggs, egg yolks, and granulated sugar and whisk until the mixture is fluffy and quite thick.

3. Add the lime zest and juice. Whisk for another minute.

4. Remove the gelatin sheets from the water and heat them up carefully in a pot until they melt. Then, mix them with a little of the egg mixture. Add the gelatin to the rest of the egg mixture.

5. In a separate bowl, whip the cream until stiff peaks form (watch that it doesn't turn into butter!).

6. Fold the cream into the egg mixture while stirring with big sweeps with a ladle or a spatula.

7. Fill either 4–6 ramekins with the mixture, or a large mold (about 1 quart / 1 liter) that has been lined with plastic wrap. Let stand in the fridge for at least 4 hours (well-covered, as the fromage can easily absorb other flavors), but preferably overnight.

8. If you are going to tip the fromage out of a large mold, you should dip the outside of the mold in lukewarm water first and then tug gently on the plastic wrap so the fromage loosens from the edges. Then it can be tipped out on a serving platter. Garnish with fruits and berries of your choice, or with nothing at all.

Merry Christmas

Christmas and New Year's leftovers

Our wallets are filled with receipts and the fridge is stuffed with leftovers. The whole family plus one or two relatives are sitting at the table, waiting to be fed. Just take it easy! You can cook many delicious and varied lunches and dinners from holiday leftovers without too much work or spending a lot. Here are our absolute best creations!

RISOTTO PANCAKES

If you have some risotto left you can make tasty little pancakes from the leftovers. Mix in an egg or two. Shape them into small pancakes. Turn them over in panko or breadcrumbs and fry them in a little butter and oil. Serve with a salad.

Pane dorato with Christmas ham

Italy's answer to hot sandwiches is a crispy cross between a sandwich and French toast. Pane dorato, golden fried bread, saves the old bread, the slightly dry ham, and the refrigerator's forgotten ends of cheese.

2 PORTIONS

a few slices of Christmas ham
approx. 2 oz (50 g) grated cheese, for example Gruyere or cheddar
strong sweet mustard
4 slices of day old bread
2 eggs
1 cups (250 ml) milk
½ tsp salt
olive oil

1. Place the ham, cheese, and mustard between two slices of bread and press them together.

2. Whisk eggs, milk, and salt in a deep dish. Dip and turn the sandwiches in the mixture.

3. Heat the oil in a frying pan. Fry the sandwiches on both sides so the cheese melts and they get a nice golden surface. Serve with a green salad.

Christmas hash

A classic hash should contain cured beef brisket, but the hash is just as delicious with Christmas ham.

4 PORTIONS

approx. 14 oz (400 g) Christmas ham
approx. 7 oz (200 g) sausage and other meat
5–6 boiled potatoes
1 yellow or red onion, peeled and finely chopped
2 tbsp butter + 2 tbsp Canola oil
salt to taste
freshly ground white pepper
Worcestershire sauce
FOR SERVING:
HP sauce, tomato ketchup, pickled beetroot, 4 fried eggs

1. Dice the ham, sausages, and potatoes.

2. Fry in butter and oil in this order: potatoes, onion, ham, and sausages. Mix it all in a bowl. Season with salt, pepper, and Worcestershire sauce.

3. Heat the hash in a microwave, frying pan, or oven.

4. Bring out the condiments and serve immediately.

Risotto with fried Christmas ham

When the ham begins to sing its last verse you can serve it fried with a creamy saffron risotto. The delicious saffron risotto can also be served at the Christmas table if you so desire.

4 PORTIONS

2 shallots
1 carrot
1 celery stalk
approx. 3¼ cups (750 ml) chicken or vegetable stock
1 tbsp butter + 1 tbsp olive oil
10½ oz (300 g) Arborio rice
½ cup (100 ml) dry white wine or cooking wine
1–2 packets of saffron
salt, freshly ground black pepper
1–2 tbsp butter
2¾ oz (75 g) grated Parmesan cheese
slightly thick slices of Christmas ham
approx. 1 tbsp butter
grated Parmesan for serving

1. Peel and finely chop the onions. Peel the carrot and cut it into thin strips or slices. Cut the celery thinly.

2. In a pot, bring the stock to a boil.

3. Heat the butter and oil in another large pot. Add in the onions and vegetables when the butter has melted. Fry until the onion is soft and transparent.

4. Add the rice and stir well so that all the kernels become shiny. Fry for a minute. Pour in the wine and bring to a boil while stirring continuously.

5. When the wine has boiled, add in the stock, one ladleful at a time. Let the stock come almost to a boil before adding the next ladleful. Stir continuously!

6. Taste the rice after about 15 minutes. The kernels should be quite soft but should still have a bit of resistance when chewed. If it feels like you're munching on chalk, it's not ready!

7. Add the saffron near the end and stir well. When the rice feels done, add salt and pepper to taste. Add in 1 tbsp of butter and the grated Parmesan. Stir well. Let stand for a couple of minutes with the lid on.

8. Fry the ham in butter until it browns a little. Serve with the risotto, a fresh salad, and grated Parmesan.

Hash browns with toppings

Serve hash browns with a variety of delicious leftovers—it's a clever use of what you've got on hand!

4 PORTIONS

3 eggs
8 potatoes
salt to taste
freshly ground white pepper
2 tbsp butter
TOPPINGS:
- bacon
- feta cheese
- ham
- a little fish roe
- finely chopped pickled herring
- sour cream
- smoked salmon
- kipper
- other tasty leftovers

1. Crack the eggs in a bowl and whisk.

2. Peel the potatoes, grate them roughly, and mix them into the egg. Add salt and pepper.

3. Prepare 3–5 of the trimmings. Fry the bacon, cut the feta cheese and ham, or whatever you have chosen.

4. Butter fry eight small hash browns a time in a hot frying pan until they are crispy on both sides.

5. Serve the hash browns on a warm tray together with small dishes of toppings.

Onion soup au gratin

When the Christmas leftovers are nearing their finish, this is both an inexpensive and fantastically delicious dinner! A wonderfully flavorful soup with a hearty blanket of bread and cheese.

4 PORTIONS

4 large onions
2 garlic cloves
3 tbsp butter
1 tsp dried thyme
3 bay leaves
¾ cup (200 ml) white wine
3½ cups (800 ml) beef stock (or vegetable stock) from bouillon cubes
salt and pepper
4 slices of day old bread
5⅓ oz (150 g) roughly grated cheese, preferably Gruyere or Emmental

1. Preheat the oven to 475°F (250°C) or set it to broil.

2. Peel and cut the onions in half. Slice the halves thinly. Peel and chop the garlic. Fry the onions and garlic in a pot together with butter, thyme, and bay leaves until soft.

3. Pour in the white wine and stock and let the soup cook for 20–30 minutes. Add salt and pepper to taste.

4. Pour the soup into small, ovenproof bowls. Dice the bread and place the pieces on the soup. Top it off with grated cheese.

5. Place the bowls on a tray and bake in the oven until the cheese has melted and browned a little.

Cheese and ham salad

A salad with Christmas ham is delicious. Here with a classic Thousand Island dressing.

4 PORTIONS

7 oz (200 g) hard cheese, aged cheddar if possible
7 oz (200 g) Christmas ham
1 small head of crispy lettuce, for example iceberg or romaine
1 red bell pepper
2 tomatoes
½ cucumber
THOUSAND ISLAND DRESSING:
¾ cup (200 ml) mayonnaise
2 tbsp tomato purée
1 tsp paprika
1 tbsp cognac
a little freshly ground white pepper
a couple of drops of red Tabasco
salt to taste
a couple of drops of lemon juice

1. Start with the dressing. Mix the mayonnaise, tomato purée, paprika, cognac, white pepper, Tabasco, and salt. Sample. Add a couple of drops of lemon juice if desired. Set the dressing aside in the fridge.

2. Slice the cheese and ham into thin strips. Wash the lettuce (place it in cold water for about an hour beforehand if it's a little wilted), dry it, and tear into smaller pieces.

3. Cut the bell pepper, tomato, and cucumber into smaller pieces.

4. Arrange everything—cheese, ham, pepper, tomato, and cucumber—prettily in a salad bowl. Serve the salad with the dressing and add some bread, if you like.

Scrambled eggs with fried pork

Soft and extra creamy scrambled eggs can be heavenly.

4 PORTIONS

8 slices of salted pork
1 tbsp butter + 1 tbsp cooking oil
10–12 cherry tomatoes
salt
3½ tbsp (50 ml) capers
SCRAMBLED EGGS:
6 eggs
2 egg yolks
½ tsp salt
2 tbsp butter
½ cup (100 ml) whipping cream

1. Fry the pork in butter and oil over medium heat so it browns nicely. Keep warm.

2. Cut the tomatoes into wedges or halves. Add salt.

3. Whisk the egg and yolks together. Add salt. Melt the butter in a pot over the lowest heat (you can also use a waterbath). Pour in the eggs and let them solidify gradually while stirring continuously with a wooden spoon or spatula.

4. When the egg begins to solidify, add the cream. Let thicken for another minute. Remove from the heat and adjust season.

5. Put the scrambled eggs on a heated plate with the pork and the tomatoes. Sprinkle capers on the pork.

Homemade shellfish broth

It's much easier to make homemade shellfish broth than most people imagine.

1 BATCH

plenty of shellfish leftovers (approx. 14 oz / 400 g)
4¼ cups (1 liter) water
¾ cup (200 ml) white wine
1 star anise
10 black peppercorns
1 bay leaf
1 clove
1 tsp dried thyme
1 tsp dill seeds, optional

1. Remove any shellfish meat and set aside (needed for the next recipe). Roast the leftover shells at 425°F (225°C) for about 20 minutes.

2. Place everything in a pot and pour in the water and the wine. Add the spices and let simmer for about 20 minutes. Strain the broth. You should now have about 3 cups (700 ml) of broth. It may not taste like a lot yet, but have patience. When it's used in a sauce, the salt and flavoring will bring out the excellent base flavor of the shellfish.

Pasta with shellfish sauce

An easy to make dish from leftovers. Creamy and flavorful.

4 PORTIONS

½ cup (100 ml) shellfish meat (see above)
1 large carrot
3½ tbsp (50 g) butter
1 tbsp tomato purée
3 cups (700 ml) shellfish broth (homemade or bouillon + water)
¾ cup (200 ml) Pernod or Ricard, optional
1 lemon, juice
salt to taste
a pinch of cayenne pepper
boiled pasta of choice

1. Dice the carrot and fry it in a little of the butter to bring out the flavor. Add tomato purée and fry for another minute.

2. Pour in the broth and liqueur and let boil for about 20 minutes so that the liquid is reduced to about 2 cups (500 ml).

3. Add lemon juice to taste as well as salt and cayenne pepper. Mix it all with the shellfish meat in a food processor or with an immersion blender. If the sauce seems too thick you can dilute it with a little water.

4. Stir in the rest of the butter just before serving. The sauce should become glossy but not perfectly smooth. Serve with pasta.

Pasta with Christmas salmon

A little leftover salmon, an onion, and a splash of cream can become a quick and lovely pasta.

4 PORTIONS

1 yellow onion or red onion
1 garlic clove
approx. 5 oz (150 g) smoked or cured salmon or gravlax
1 tbsp olive oil + 1 tbsp butter
¾ cup (200 ml) whipping cream
freshly ground black pepper
salt
a pinch of cayenne pepper
lemon juice
cooked pasta of choice
boiled vegetables
chopped herbs, roasted nuts, and breadcrumbs, optional

1. Peel and finely chop the onion and garlic. Cut the salmon into fine strips.

2. Fry the onion and garlic in butter and oil for a couple of minutes without browning. Add the salmon and pour in the cream. Let simmer for a couple of minutes. Season with black pepper, salt, cayenne pepper, and maybe a little lemon juice.

3. Serve with pasta and boiled vegetables. Sprinkle with chopped herbs, roasted pistachios or other nuts, and breadcrumbs fried crispy in olive oil.

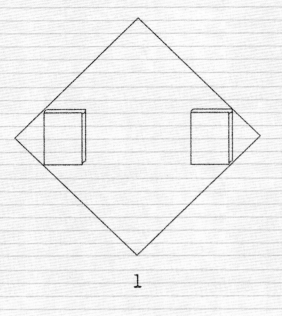

1

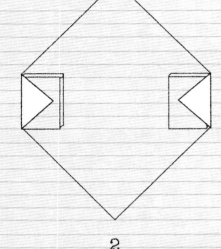

2

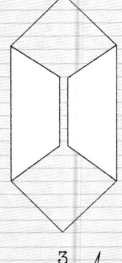

3

4

5

FUROSHIKI

Japanese wrapping with fabric to give two books as Christmas gifts.

You need: A not too coarse, square piece of fabric, about 28 x 28 in (70 x 70 cm)—a remnant piece, a pretty scarf or some other attractive fabric. Make sure that the fabric has been ironed before you start wrapping the books.

1. Place the fabric diagonally in front of you, with one corner pointing toward you. Place the books in the middle of the fabric opposite each other, with space between them.

2. Grab both corners and fold them inward on top of the books.

3. Fold in the fabric and books one more time toward each other and scoot the books toward the center. Make sure to stretch the fabric so that any wrinkles disappear.

4. Cross the upper and lower parts of the fabric across the middle of the bundle. Twine the ends around each other another time.

5. Fold the entire bundle in the middle. Tie the two loose fabric ends together into a handle.

PAPER STARS

You need: 5 square sheets of paper, about 8 x 8 in (20 x 20 cm), tape, stapler.

1. Fold the paper diagonally into a triangle.

2. Cut ten strips from the folded edge in toward the middle (follow the diagram). Save a strip in the center, the strips are supposed to be attached in the middle.

3. Unfold the sheet. Lift up and tape together the corner of the inner square so that a tube is formed. Rotate the sheet and lift and tape together the corners of the next square. Rotate the sheet again and do the same with the next corner, etc.

4. Make a total of five of these shapes. Place the ends of the five shapes together and staple together. Then, staple the sides together as well so you get a star.

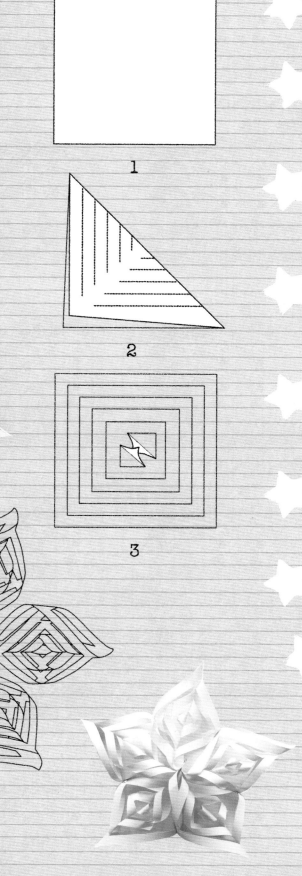

1

2

3

4

Index

Jens and Johanna wish to thank:

Wise, talented, and warm Ulrika Pousette who took the fantastic photographs. Beautiful, careful, and inventive Emilie Crispin Ekström for the design. The stellar Pia Koskela for the very cool and wonderful collages. The publisher's Sara Nyström and Anna Paljak for their industrious work, good advice, and merry calls.

The City Mission on Hantverkargatan for all the props that we borrowed. House Doctor, PUB, for lending us a variety of bits and pieces. Skansen which lent us the lucia crown. Ylva Bergqvist for lending us props. Emilie's uncle Robert who lent us his couch. Coast, NK, for lending us dresses. Grönsakshallen, Sorunda, and Ekofisk. Loveliest Karolina Sparring for excellent salmon recipes. Gunilla Wetterlundh, Carin Ståhlberg, Elin Peters, and Måns Wahlgren. Åke Nordgren and Björn Westlund. Santa Claus.

Jens would also like to thank:

Johanna Linder, Ivar, Otto, and the rest of my family and relations for all the lovely Christmases in Bollmora, Halmstad, Sandviken, Trosa, and Sättersta. Especially my mother Lena and grandmother Ella and her sister Ann-Britt for teaching me to cook everything from kale to Christmas cookies. Thank you also to Stefan Wettainen.

Johanna would also like to thank:

My brothers and mother and father for more than 40 wonderful Christmases together, for many of the dishes in the book and for all our highly valued traditions. My lovely family—Erik, Greta, Bobo, and Svante who put up with celebrating Christmas year round. Because you sample most things with a happy face and help with decorations and baking.

Notes

Notes

Notes

Notes

Notes

Notes

Notes

Notes